you
are the light

Rediscovering the Eastern Jesus

you
are the light

John Martin Sahajananda

BOOKS

Winchester, UK
New York, USA

Copyright © 2003 O Books
46A West Street, Alresford, Hants SO24 9AU, UK
Tel: +44 (0) 1962 736880 Fax: +44 (0) 1962 736881
E-mail: office@johnhunt-publishing.com
www.0-books.net

US office:
240 West 35th Street, Suite 500
New York, NY10001
E-mail: obooks@aol.com

Text: © John Martin Sahajananda 2003
Cover design: © Echelon Design
Typography: Jim Weaver Design

ISBN 1 903816 30 0

Reprinted 2004, 2005

A CIP catalogue record for this book is available from the British Library.

Printed in Dubai by Oriental Press

Contents

PART THREE
A new Christianity

PART FOUR
The Hindu-Christian experience of God

O God will I ever be first?
*I began to come to you
But I found you coming to me.
I wanted to run to you
But I found you running to me.
I wanted to wait for you
But I found you waiting for me.
I wanted to search for you
But I found you searching for me.
I thought I found you
But I was found by you.
I wanted to say 'I love you'
But I heard you say 'I love you'.
I wanted to choose you
But you have chosen me.
I wanted to write to you
But I received your letter.
I wanted to live in you
But I found you living in me.
I wanted to ask your forgiveness
But I found you forgiving me.
I wanted to offer myself to you
But I found you offering yourself to me.
I wanted to offer friendship to you
But I found you offering your friendship to me.
I wanted to call you 'Abba, Father' first
But I heard you calling 'My Son' first.
I wanted to reveal my inner life to you
But I found you revealing your inner life to me.
I wanted to invite you into my life
But I received your invitation into your life.
I wanted to rejoice over my return
But I found you rejoicing over my return.*
O God, WILL I EVER BE FIRST?

Dedicated to

The Trinity of Shantivanam

Fr Jules Monchanin
(Swami Parama Arupiananda)

Fr Henri le Saux
(Swami Abishiktananda)

Fr Bede Griffiths
(Swami Dayananda)

Foreword

Ever since my childhood I have always been told that Jesus Christ came to proclaim the good news to humanity. Our sacred scriptures are called 'Good News'. But as I grew I could not really understand what this good news of Jesus was about as what I was taught focused almost entirely on having to believe in certain propositions and in particular events.

The answers I got from the Christian tradition failed to convince me and all the divisions within Christianity disturbed me greatly. This made me a passionate seeker of the good news of Jesus, both existentially and theologically. I eventually stumbled upon a revolutionary answer to my questions. I realized that the Christian tradition has yet to discover this good news of Jesus.

The good news is not something about God, Jesus or a new religion but it is about the dignity of human beings. I discovered that the core of Jesus' message is that human beings are greater than religions. This reality is expressed in the well-known statement, 'I am the way, the truth and the life'.

Jesus summarized his good news in one sentence: 'The kingdom of God is at hand, repent.' This good news reveals where God is and where human beings are, who God is and who human beings are. It reveals that God is everywhere and human beings are living and moving in God just as fish live and move in the ocean. It reveals that God and human beings are ultimately one, just as the water and the ice, although they are experienced as separate, are ultimately one. This understanding that God and creation are not two separate realities is revealed in the famous statement of Jesus, 'I and the Father are one'.

Unfortunately human beings, out of ignorance, and not realising that they already are in God, have created ways and means, that we call religions, to 'reach' God. In this way humanity has erected an artificial wall between God and human beings who have then become the slaves of their own creation. Jesus came to announce the good news and liberate people from this ignorance and slavery.

The message of Jesus is universally valid. It unites humanity and it liberates human beings from the oppression of belief structures. The message of Jesus ultimately opens up the possibility for men and women to enter into the highest divine-human relationship.

When I look at the world today in which traditional Christianity is losing her hold I see that many Christians are moving towards other religious traditions for their spiritual needs. Indeed some speak of 'post-Christianity'. People see that Jesus Christ is not only a source of division among different religions but also among Christians themselves. At the same time many faithful Christians are trying to understand the deeper meaning of the good news of Jesus and its relevance for our times and I feel an existential need to share with my fellow Christians, and with all people of good will, this liberating message of Christ, which brings peace between religions and amongst Christians themselves.

The problem is that human beings are serving religions

rather than religions serving human beings. The message of Jesus actually focuses on the primacy of human beings. It actually breaks down the walls of division and creates one God and one humankind. Today sharing the good news of Jesus is to announce the dignity of human beings, all of whom have the potential to transcend religions and 'ways' to God and declare boldly, 'I am the way, the truth and the life'.

I would like to extend my heartfelt respects to the founders of Shantivanam, Fr Jules Monchanin, Fr Henri Le Saux and Fr Bede Griffiths, whose life and writings have been a great source of inspiration. Father Bede brought about a revolution in my spiritual path and had been my spiritual master for nine years when he died in 1993. I owe much to the place of Shantivanam where I have been living since 1984. It is in Shantivanam that I experienced the flow of divine love and inspiration and where I produced most of my writings.

I am also grateful to my brothers at Shantivanam and at Camaldoli, in Italy, who have encouraged my spiritual search. I cannot forget the support and encouragement I received from Sr Jeanne Van Hacht (Sr Mechtildes), who now lives in Belgium and who has been a guide, a critic, a benefactor, a mother and above all a good friend. I also remember my eldest sister Jojamma who has a special place in my heart. It was her loving act that made me what I am today. Also my younger brother-priest Fr K. Balajoji who has also been a constant source of support and encouragement.

The present work is a collection of articles I have written for different occasions and it is possible that there might be some repetitions here and there. I have to thank Nicolas Dewey who first put into my mind the possibility of publishing my writings as an anthology in the West and who vigorously pursued this idea. He has been a constant source of support and encouragement and he offered his professional help in editing the book together with Adrian Rance. The members of Bede Griffiths' Sangha in the UK, and its coordinators and personal friends, Adrian Rance and Jill Hemmings, have given me wholehearted support and encouragement even in times of difficulty and uncertainty. Adrian has generously accepted the task of reading through the material and making it readable for Western readers. He has spent considerable time on it with dedication and affection. He also took responsibility for finding a publisher, with success. May the Lord bless him abundantly. I have to thank Shirley de Boulay for reading Adrian's initial manuscript and giving valuable suggestions, which resulted in considerable improvements. I would also like to thank Jane Saunderson, Sighle Mary O'Donoghue, and Joan Walters whose friendship, affection and support have been a source of support and help. I would like to thank everyone who is directly or indirectly involved in publishing this book even if his or her name is not mentioned.

My special thanks go to Mr John Hunt, of John Hunt Publishing who kindly came forward to publish this book. His personal warmth and appreciation are very much remembered.

Br K. John Martin Sahajananda
Shantivanam
August 2002

Preface

Three wise men from the West

This book is dedicated to the three founding fathers of Saccidananda Ashram. The ashram, better known as Shantivanam (literally Forest of Peace), is near the small village of Tannirpalli, on the banks of the sacred River Cavery, about 30 kilometers from the southern Indian city of Trichy. It was founded in 1950 by two French priests, Jules Monchanin and Henri le Saux, and later achieved a worldwide reputation as a place of prayer and inter-religious dialog under the inspiration and leadership of Bede Griffiths, an English Benedictine monk who came to the ashram in 1968.

These founding fathers of Shantivanam can be thought of as three wise men from the West, the modern day counterparts of the three wise men of the East who came to worship and offer gifts to the infant Jesus. The three wise men from the East came searching for the child Jesus born from above and, being wise, they saw the limitations of their minds and their knowledge, and looked into the sky for the star of wisdom to appear. The journey of the wise men represents the collective and individual journey of humanity, the journey of our human search for truth. They began their journey in the East and they ended it in the spiritual 'east' that is, in God, in eternity, the source of Life, the eternal Word.

But the human mind then reduced the eternal Word revealed in the stable to the God and Father of Jesus Christ and in so doing divided Christians from non-Christians and closed the door to the God of eternity. God the Father of Jesus Christ is the God of memory and tradition and not the God of eternity. As we shall see in this book, all religions, including Christianity, are based on the God of memory, but it is the direct experience of God alone that can break down the barriers caused in the name of the God of memory and heal the wounds of division in our world. In the Indian tradition religions are seen as *apara vidhya* or inferior wisdom but the teachings of Jesus were built on the foundation of *para vidhya*, the direct experience of God.

Today Christians are divided in the name of Christ and Christ is a source of division between the world religions. Ecumenism and inter-religious dialog, although they have some value, seek unity in our memories, in scriptures and traditions but this is looking for the living among the dead. The past cannot unite us – it is only the God of the future who can unite humanity. The call of God to men and women of today is to look for and discover the God of eternity, to return to their original source and to seek the virgin and the inner cave, the stable made by God and not by the human mind. This is a call to a radical discontinuity from the past and, as we shall see, the wise men, the virgin and the child in the Christmas story all represent, are symbolic of, this discontinuity with the past.

This is the context in which we can understand God's call to the founders of Shantivanam. The three wise men of the Christmas story came from the geographic East, and ended their journey in the spiritual 'east' where there they saw the rising sun of the birth of Christ. Almost two thousand years later

God then asked three wise men, the founding fathers of our ashram, to journey from the West to the East, both in an actual and in a spiritual sense. The founders of Shantivanam were wise men; they all had profound knowledge of their tradition and had lived it deeply for many years. But they were not satisfied. They all saw the limitation of their Christian tradition and felt something was lacking. This is the realization that makes one a virgin, a child, and wise, for with these qualities one can listen to the call of God and make the journey to the spiritual 'east', the source of inner being, the virgin land within. For all three this call was an interior call, a journey into the cave of the heart where the encounter with the living God takes place. Having learnt about God through tradition and the scriptures, Jules Monchanin, Henri le Saux and Bede Griffiths were called to encounter God directly.

These holy men were called to make this journey in an external sense to India in whose culture there is acceptance that men and women must seek the source of life. Perhaps India was chosen because it would be here that the child born to these virgins could be better nourished and protected. Perhaps they saw that in the West religion had become like Herod, preoccupied with preserving power, position and continuity; Herod did not want new creative ideas that might be a threat and just as an angel told Joseph to take Mary and the child to Egypt and remain there until the child became strong enough to confront the king and the priest, so the virgins of the West were called to go to India until the Lord called them back in spirit or in person.

The meeting of the virgin, the child and the wise men took place in an insignificant place, a stable in which animals lived. The Eternal Word, born in obscurity to an insignificant woman in an insignificant cattle shed, in an insignificant land under military occupation, became the saviour of humanity. In the same way our founding fathers were guided to a place called Tannirpalli, a small village as obscure and insignificant as the stable of Bethlehem, a place whose name does not even appear on the map of India. Their hermitages in the ashram were more like stables than houses, and it was in this obscurity that they were called to give birth to the Eternal Word, which now has become a prophetic word for our times.

The sages who came from the West to the East in turn became prophets from the East to the West. The word delivered by them became a word that healed. The authenticity of this word was its universal validity, its unifying quality, its liberating power, its possibility for human growth and its reasonable persuasion. Their word was and is authentic because it was prophetic and liberating. The word announced by the founding fathers of Shantivanam breaks down the walls of division and creates one God and one humanity. It reveals universal wisdom, the Eternal Logos, which has manifested itself in human history but which also transcends it.

Like many seekers of God in India, Henri le Saux, who took the name Abishiktananda, came to India and made a pilgrimage to Gangotri, the source of the Ganges, the most holy river in India. In the same way every person is invited to make a pilgrimage to their spiritual 'east' and to the source of life, for the journey to the source of life is true conversion, repentance, true rebirth. The original water of God running in the conduit of time is contaminated and conditioned by history; it has lost its freshness and vitality. There is a continuous need to return to the source of life, but only wise men and women who have seen the limitations of the conditioned waters, the limitations of religious tradition, can make this journey. The king and the priest, preoccupied in protecting the continuity of their tradition and power, are afraid of the original waters. Only people who have become dissatisfied with the waters of the village and who have a profound desire for the living waters will go, like John the Baptist, into the desert to listen to the Word.

The spiritual journeys of the founders of our ashram can be understood in the light of the spiritual tradition of India, which describes human life as being in four stages. The first two of the four states are *Brahmacharya*, in which the student learns about *Brahman* as revealed in the scriptures and *Grhastha*, in which one takes responsibility in society. These two stages belong to the level of continuity, which is essential to maintain order in society. The third stage is that of *Vanaprastha*, the hermitical life, in which is the beginning of the process of discontinuity. This stage is a movement from the external to the internal and is when one starts 'digging the well within'. The fourth stage is the state of *Sannyasa*, the supreme state of discontinuity. Whereas the *brahmachari* and *grhastha* follow the law of tradition and continuity, the hermit and the *sannyasi* follow the law of discontinuity. A *sannyasi* is not bound by tradition and lives according to the *Sanathana Dharma*, the eternal will of God. His way of life is the way of death, dying to the past and moving into the eternal present. He has to be always on the move and cannot settle down.

Our founding fathers lived the first two stages in the West where they learned from their tradition as *brahmacharis* and lived their tradition seriously and profoundly as priests and monks, as *grhastas*. Then they began their journey as hermits and, at its culmination, as *sannyasis*. The beauty of their journey was that it brought the two traditions of East and West together. These three wise men from the West were guided by the star of wisdom to the stable of Shantivanam, they were open to the spiritual 'east' as the symbol of Eternity and were able to build a bridge between the God of history and the God of Eternity. In the stable of Shantivanam they found the Word who transcends Christian churches, and all religions, and transcends both ecumenism and inter-religious dialog. This obscure place in India is the external symbol of an internal 'stable' where God or truth is born. Shantivanam is the symbol of our inner being where the boundaries disappear. Where there are no boundaries there is the forest of peace, Shantivanam.

The call of God to Jules Monchanin, Henri le Saux and Bede Griffiths is the call of God to every man and woman to become a spiritual virgin, to become a child, to become a wise person, to be reborn, to make the pilgrimage to the source of life, the interior and spiritual 'east'.

Introduction

My encounter with God

Looking back I realize that from an early age my life had been moving in a definite direction, leading up to the moment I felt the touch of God. I was born in the Indian state of Andhra Pradesh to a poor family, the sixth child of my parents. It was my father who first taught me to pray and it was from him that I learnt the rosary. Often as a child, without him knowing, I would see him praying alone, silently in a solitary place, and from him I learnt the habit of now and then praying alone. Even today I can visualize the scene.

My early life was hard and in my youth I had to face many difficulties. Now I am convinced that God brought all these difficulties upon me to teach me his love and concern. The way of God is strange and I can see now that God loved me so much that he made me suffer so that I would realize that he loved me. My school life was hard. In my sixth standard I had to stop studying for a year due to my mother's ill health, but then I started again with the help of my eldest sister. Unfortunately she got married the following year, leaving me alone and desolate in a poor boys' hostel. I could attend only half of the classes in my seventh standard, but despite this I managed to get through the exams. In my eighth standard I was asked to leave the hostel, as I could not pay the hostel fees, so I had to go back home to my native place, where I was forced to work without any hope of further study. But God has his own plans, and one day I received a letter from the hostel warden asking me to come back and take my final exams. After that I was asked by my parents to get my transfer certificate so that I could continue my studies back home at my native place, where I was able to finish my ninth and tenth classes. But finally, at the age of 15, I had to discontinue my studies to support the family.

After that darkness again entered my life. For four long years the burden of the whole family fell upon me and I had to work in an oil factory, all day and sometimes at night. When there was no work at the factory I used to find other work. I had no hope of further study and was sure that I would end my life as a daily laborer. It was then that I learnt what it meant to be a worker and a paid laborer.

One evening, after four years of this work I got a letter from my eldest sister together with an application form for an intermediate course at a junior college. The letter came when all the colleges were closed except for this one, which had obtained permission to start a new section. When my parents expressed their wish that I should go to the college, I laughed and said, 'What are you saying? I have forgotten everything, please I cannot study now. Don't send me.' But they insisted, even though I wept, and I had to go to the college. When the principal saw my tenth class certificate and found that I had not studied for four years he advised me to join in an industrial school. But I was silent. Anyhow, he gave me the place and luckily I got second-class in my intermediate, which surprised him.

My difficulties did not come to an end with this. After the intermediate examination, what was I to do? My parents could not support my studies any more. It was a big question. Luckily I got a place at the Silver Jubilee College, Kurnool, where we were given a stipend of one hundred rupees per month together with board and lodging. Without this I could not have continued my studies. God's hand was upon me.

When I realized that I had the chance to study again my joy knew no bounds. It was a resurrection from death. From that day I saw that I should not waste this precious life, and that I should live it fully and meaningfully. I had a vague idea of joining the seminary so that I could serve God and my fellow men. I prayed to God, 'Lord, you have given me new life, please give me also a task to perform.' I had tried to join a seminary after my intermediate but I had not been successful. I tried again having taken my degree and this time the doors were open to me.

I was very happy to go to the minor seminary. However as the days passed it turned into a horrible experience. Until then I had seen the priesthood from the outside and now I was seeing it from within. I was seeing the world from the other side and began to hear complaints against priests and the religious and even bishops. I slowly began to understand what it means to be a priest. To give up married life? To give up everything? To be away from parents, relatives and friends? Why should I be the one to sacrifice for the sake of God and others? Before this I had been very prayerful but now I could not pray peacefully. Once I had thanked God and praised him for his favors and mercies towards me; now I began to doubt even his existence. The world's problems became my problems. I saw God as being responsible for every evil in the world.

I was 25 years old in December 1980 when I went to the major seminary and it was here that I hoped that I would get all the answers. I had ample opportunity to read many books, and in the first year of my life there I felt so close to God it was as if he was leading me step by step. But as I began to study philosophy, all my ideas of God began to break down. My understanding of God appeared to be without foundation, and from my own experience, and the experiences of other people, I realized that we cannot prove the existence of God. So we have to believe in him first. Faith is the foundation of religion.

As I began to read philosophy my mind turned to the most fundamental philosophical questions. Why should we believe in God? What is the necessity of God in our lives? What is prayer? What is the effect of prayer in our lives? Can't we live without God and without prayer as do millions of people? Is God necessary in this secular and scientific world in which most of our lives are conditioned by the laws of the state? For the first time I realized how the human mind questions everything when it is about to give up something of its own. It is not when we have everything that we find the meaning of our life, but when we are about to lose everything.

I had the opportunity to learn about many other religious beliefs and practices. I did not read them as a spectator but as an actor, involving myself in them and reading them as one who was ready to accept whatever was true in them. I studied Indian philosophy, existentialism, Marxism and other major philosophical ideologies. I did not study them simply for the sake of passing exams but rather in the hope that they could solve the problems burning in my heart. But none of these systems could provide the solutions I sought. Even my own religious convictions were very hard to understand without faith.

I became a traveler standing at the crossroads not knowing which way to go. No road was able to satisfy me or convince me. It was a horrible experience. I understood how all these philosophers must have suffered as they sought solutions to their problems. I lost all hope and confidence in philosophy. It could not answer my questions and could not give certainty. I also realized that science could not answer my questions because what I sought was not an object of scientific investigation. It belonged to an invisible reality. I also lost hope in theology, which appeared to be merely defending what one believed (what one had already decided to do and not to do).

All the books I read created new problems instead of solving any, and so I lost faith in searching for answers in books of philosophy, science and theology. I did not know what to do. But there was a burning fire in me still asking the question about what it means to live. From the beginning I was convinced that life was more than studying, more than getting a job, getting a high position, or getting fame and fortune. It was more than marrying and having children. So I gave up looking for answers to my questions outside of myself. I decided that I had to find the reason to live, and the reason to die, not in books, not outside, but within myself.

Prayer had always been an important part of my life. I never gave up praying, for when I was praying I felt near to the unfathomable, invisible reality. Now I began to improve my prayer life thinking that it might at least dampen the burning fire in me. But the more I began to pray the thirstier I felt. I spent hours and hours in prayer, and I read books on prayer and tried to practice as many methods as possible. But no method could satisfy me; I discussed God and the effect of prayer with many people, but their answers did not satisfy me. I found that for many people religion was only an obligation, they did not have any personal conviction, whereas some had lost their faith in God, which they considered more as an obstacle to their progress and freedom. Others prayed to God to get something from him and others feared that if they didn't pray God might get angry and punish them.

I realized again that I could not find the solution to all my problems outside myself. I was the source of all these problems; they were coming out of me so the answer must be within me. I did not want to believe simply because others believed. For me life was so precious and important I wanted to take all pre-cautions before investing in any bank. If the bank in which I invested turned out to be a false one or went bankrupt I felt I would lose my life. It was this fear that made me consider the true meaning and purpose of my life and want to live it fully and sincerely. At the same time I realized that I could not always be searching and that if I wanted to live I had to stop searching. I felt that searching precedes living and that I was not living so long as I was searching.

My search for true prayer was the answer to all my questions, both philosophical and theological. I had this strong inclina-tion towards personal prayer that I had learnt from watching my father praying alone. I used to have a picture of Jesus in front of me on my table and I would speak with him, face to face, pouring out all my problems before him, and I would feel comforted. That was my everyday prayer. But when I started my seminary life I started to go deep into my prayer life. It started with intercessory prayer and later went to meditative prayer. The stage came when I could not utter a word; I simply used to sit before the tabernacle without saying anything. However, each night before I went to bed I would say my personal prayer for 15 minutes. I would open the Gospel and said, 'Speak, Lord, for your servant is listening.' I would read a passage from the Gospel and pour out all my problems to Jesus. One day, during this time of personal prayer, I got a strange idea. I asked myself, 'Martin, you pray to God every day asking for the many things which you need. Now you have all the material necessities possible. You don't need anything, except maybe a position in the future, but that is all. If you don't have to ask God for anything why don't you ask God if he needs anything from you?' I laughed at the idea that God might need anything from me.

So one day before going to bed I sat before the picture of Jesus and prayed like this, though I was laughing at my strange notion. I said, 'Lord, you have given me enough to eat four times a day whereas millions of my brothers and sisters are starving, unable to get even one full meal a day. You have given me four sets of clothing whereas millions of my brothers and sisters live half-naked. You have given me a nice room to stay in whereas millions of my brothers and sisters live on sidewalks and in slums. You have given me good health whereas millions of my brothers and sisters are suffering from physical and mental illness. You have given me good parents, brothers, sisters and friends whereas millions of my brothers and sisters are orphans, friendless and deserted. You have given me freedom whereas millions of my brothers and sisters are living behind bars without the hope of being free. You have given me a good education whereas millions of my brothers and sisters live in ignorance. O Lord I am ashamed to ask anything more for myself. Lord do you want me to do anything for you? Lord what do you want me to do for you?'

This was the turning point of my life. I do not know how long God had been waiting for me to ask this question, but he caught hold of me. I began to pray in this way for some days and the answer I found was to 'know the will of God'. How to know the will of God? To know his will is to listen to his voice. How do you listen to his voice and find out his will and then do it?

One evening I was going for a walk when something unusual happened to me. Whenever I walked out I would come across many beggars asking for help and I would feel pity for them, and give whatever I could give. But on this occasion a girl of 10 years came up to me, stretched out her hand with an empty bowl, begging for something. Her condition was pathetic. Her eyes had sunk inside their sockets. Her stomach was empty, as if she had not eaten properly for days. With her torn clothes she was half naked. Her bowl was empty. Confronted by this a new revelation came to me.

In front of her empty bowl I found myself with pockets full of money.

In front of her empty stomach I found myself with a full stomach.

In front of her insecure life, living on the footpaths, I found myself living a secure life with all the luxuries.

In front of her orphaned and uncared for life, I found myself in a well cared for life.

In front of her half naked body I found myself with clothes and fully covered.

Then I felt a kind of call:

> The empty bowl is calling to the full pockets, 'Fill me.'
> The empty stomach is calling to the full stomach, 'Feed me.'
> The insecure life is calling to the well-secured life, 'Give me security.'
> The uncared for life is calling to the well cared for life, 'Care for me, love me.'
> The half naked body is calling to the fully covered body, 'Cover me.'

The material emptiness was calling to the material fullness, but the material fullness had no life to flow spontaneously. I did not know what to do. I felt myself standing like a criminal in front of a judge who was condemning me.

> Your pockets are responsible for my empty bowl.
> Your huge buildings are responsible for my desolate life on the footpaths.
> Your cared for life is responsible for my uncared for life.
> Your well-dressed body is responsible for my nakedness.
> You are responsible. You are responsible. You are the criminal.
> You are the criminal.

My ears resounded with these words. I felt as if she was the prophetess sent by God to open my eyes. I could not bear any more. I took two rupees from my pocket and placed it into the empty bowl of the little girl. When the girl saw the two rupees there was joy in her face. She slowly turned and started going. But I still heard the words, even as she left:

> You are responsible. You are responsible. You are the criminal.
> You are the criminal.

This was not just an encounter between the little girl and me. It was an encounter between two classes of society of which we were only the representatives. As an individual I came from a poor family but as a seminarian I belonged to the official church, I was rich. It was an encounter between the rich and the poor, between the powerful and the powerless, the able and the disabled, the masters and the slaves, the secure and the insecure, the employer and the employee. It made a deep impression on me. I felt as though millions of these helpless people were standing on the side of the road, mocking me, saying, 'See here goes the criminal. See, here goes the criminal!' Even today whenever I see a beggar I hear the same words.

That evening I began to reflect on the incident. Am I responsible for the suffering of my millions of brothers and sisters in this world? I slowly realized that I am responsible for them, because I am not an isolated individual but part and parcel of a system that exists. In choosing my own options, either political or economic, I choose for the whole of humanity and not just for myself. My decisions, my choices, my options affect the lives of my fellow human beings. I realized I had been committing a mortal sin against my fellow human beings by separating myself from them.

When the time came for my personal prayer I sat before the picture of Jesus and asked the same question. 'Lord, what do you want me to do for you?' That day the answer was very clear, 'Allow me to enter you so that I may fill the empty bowl, feed the empty stomach, clothe the naked bodies. That I may give security to the insecure, love the uncared for and the unloved.'

I had not expected this reply. To allow God to work in me was the most terrible request that I had ever faced in my life. I did not know how to respond. Suddenly I found myself in the presence of God and the spirit of God surrounded me like a flood asking me to open the door of my heart, the keys of which I possessed, so that he could enter into me and work in me and through me.

Then a new revelation and awareness came to me. I suddenly became like that little girl whom I met on the road; I turned into a beggar with an empty bowl in my hand. I found myself with an empty stomach starving for spiritual food. I found myself with the nakedness of sinfulness, trying to cover myself and to hide from the presence of God. I found myself traveling in a boat that was sinking.

The little girl stood begging, asking for something; God

stood giving, offering me something. But there was an irony in God's giving, in his offering, for it implied:

Your spiritual bowl is empty, let me fill it.

Your spiritual stomach is hungry, starving, let me feed it.

You are spiritually insecure, your spiritual boat is sinking, let me give you security.

You are spiritually naked, sinful, let me cover you, clothe you.

This was both dreadful and unexpected. I felt like a millionaire who had turned into a beggar overnight, like a man who traveled the whole day at 100 kilometers per hour and then found he was going in the wrong direction. I found myself like a man whose boat was sinking in the middle of the sea; I felt like a man who drank alcohol only to discover that it was poison.

I felt so much anguish and bitterness that I cried out, 'Lord, you have deceived me. Lord, you have deceived me. You are like a friend who walked alongside me but then suddenly took a knife from his pocket and stood in front of me to steal my belongings. O Lord, I am a sinner. I am living in a sinful world.' I stood before God like a criminal caught red-handed and standing in front of the police with no chance of escape. I accepted, saying, 'Lord, I am a criminal. I am a criminal.' I felt I had been living for 25 years without living, that I had been praying for 25 years without praying, because what I had been doing reflected only my own values.

I realized that this encounter was not between me and God alone, but between God and the whole of humanity. I was not standing before God as an individual, but I was standing on the foundation of all the philosophical systems, political parties and religious systems of the world. In my encounter the little girl condemned me by begging, by asking for something, but now God condemned me by offering, by giving me something. We have built barriers between God and human beings and between one human being and another human being.

There was no alternative. I either had to allow God in and live, or keep him out and die. But to open the door was not easy. The door, which separates me from God is not an ordinary door, the sort that can be opened once and left; it is a spring door, which stays open only as long as we hold it, but once we open the door we have no choice but to hold it open as long as we live. So I asked God to give me the strength to open the door and to keep it open throughout my life. I could not refuse because to allow God to work in me is the point of my human existence. God reveals himself in revealing what we are. God is like a mirror in which we see who we are. With this realization it was as if I was standing in front of Jesus hearing him say, 'The Kingdom of God is within you. Repent', that is, turn within yourself and discover.

It was then that I understood the message of Jesus that God is living in the depths of my heart, that I had to enter into him or allow him to enter into me. I opened the door of my heart and found the spirit of God entering like a flood, and my joy knew no bounds. I wanted to go out of my room and shout out loud, 'I have found the Kingdom of God. I have found God!' But I was afraid people would think I had gone mad. My joy was like the joy of a beggar winning a million rupees in a lottery. It was like the joy of a man caught up in a flood who sees a helicopter coming to rescue him. It was just like the joy of a man condemned to death but suddenly freed. It was just like the joy of a person dying of thirst in the desert finding water. The immeasurable riches, the Kingdom of God, that is God, which I had found in my life, was something no man in the world could have given me. It was something that I could not buy had

I all the riches of the world, and that no one in the world could take away from me.

All my doubts vanished. All the philosophy and theology that I had studied became meaningful and I could see everything in the new light of the Kingdom of God. I had thought God was somewhere in heaven, sitting with his angels. Now I realized that he is very close to us. He is within us.

I realized that this treasure is not given to me alone but to the whole world, from the beginning of creation up to the end. Every human being has this treasure of the Kingdom of God within himself or herself. The great truth that I had found was that it was God who found me. In my searching for God I discovered that God was searching for me. Truth is like a circle. We come to the place from where we started. Humanity might be disappointed to discover it is marching to where it started or rather to where it fell, but we are marching towards the end and returning to the beginning. The beginning and the end are identical.

Part **1**

The Good News of Jesus Christ

In Possession of Truth
One day I saw the Truth
shining like a bright star.
It was very small and
I could see it fully.
'How great I am
I can see the Truth fully,' I thought.
'Let me go and possess it,' I decided.
I began my journey
in possession of Truth.
As I journeyed days and days
my enthusiasm grew greater.
I felt I was closer to it
and the day to possess it is not far.
But as I walked further
I found a great change.
The closer I came
the bigger the star grew.
I journeyed and journeyed
until I was surrounded by it.
I lifted my head to the sky
and found myself under the radiance of the star.
I could see neither its beginning nor its end.
I stood there motionless without knowing
where to go.
Whichever side I saw I found its radiance.
When I started it was smaller than me,
now it is bigger than me.
When I started it was outside me
now I am inside it.
I started in possession of it

now I found myself possessed by it.
I never knew the Truth appears small
When we are far away from it.

Chapter 1

The Good News

A friend once said to me, 'You Christians say that Jesus Christ came to announce the Good News. Can you tell me what is the Good News that Jesus proclaimed to humanity?' I realized that I could not answer my friend's question, and this realization was an important moment in my spiritual journey.

What does it mean when we say that Jesus announced the Good News of the kingdom of God? In the Gospel of Mark we read that after the arrest of John the Baptist Jesus came to Galilee:

> Preaching the good news of the Kingdom of God and saying, 'The time is fulfilled, the kingdom of God is at hand, repent and believe in the gospel.'[1]

Similarly in the Gospel of Matthew we read that from that time Jesus began to preach, 'Repent, for the kingdom of heaven is at hand.'[2] So Jesus preached a simple message in three parts, the 'kingdom of God', 'at hand', and 'repent'. If these three statements are understood correctly then the whole gospel is understood. If these three statements are misinterpreted then the whole of the gospel is misinterpreted.

The phrase 'kingdom of God' and 'kingdom of heaven' mean the same thing. Matthew, writing to the Jewish Christians, uses the more reverential term 'heaven' as Jews did not address God directly but used substitutes. For instance, phrases found in the Gospels such as 'give us a sign from above', and 'unless you are born from above', the word 'above' is used as a substitute for God. Mark was writing for the Christians in Rome and he did not have such reservations.

The essence of Jesus' message to humanity is 'The kingdom of God is at hand, repent,' and the rest of the Gospels are only a working out of this one great sentence. If we understand this one statement we can understand everything else that Jesus said. Jesus announced his message as the *Good News*. Good news immediately makes us happy. For instance if a student gets the news that he or she has passed an exam, or if someone hears that they have won a million pounds in the lottery, both of these events are received as good news. It is the same when an incurably sick person comes to know that someone has discovered a treatment for his or her condition, or when a mother who has lost her child hears that the child is found. Jesus announced Good News that must have made people happy *as soon as they heard it.*

So what was this Good News? The phrase 'kingdom of God' is a technical term and has been interpreted in various ways in the Christian tradition. Initially it was taken to mean a political kingdom. The Jews lived under Roman occupation and expected a Messiah who would deliver them from this oppression and establish God's rule in Palestine. Some people thought that Jesus would establish an earthly kingdom and rule as King David had ruled in days of old. Jesus was actually tempted by this aspiration and the devil took him to a very high mountain and showed him all the kingdoms of the world in all their greatness and said, 'All this I give to you if you kneel down and worship me.'[3] But Jesus rejected the temptation. Again, when Jesus multiplied the bread, people wanted to make him a king by force, but Jesus 'went away from them'.[4] Even his own disciples thought that Jesus would establish an earthly kingdom. The mother of the sons of Zebedee came to Jesus asking that her sons might sit at the right side and left side of Jesus.[5] When Jesus told his disciples that the Son of Man had to suffer and be killed, Peter reacted strongly and said, 'Lord this will never happen to you,' but Jesus told him, 'Get behind me Satan, you are not on the side of God but of men.'[6] The disciples on the road to Emmaus said to one another, 'and we had hoped that he would be the one who was going to set Israel free.'[7] Again, after the resurrection the disciples asked Jesus, 'Lord, will you at this time give the kingdom back to Israel?' but Jesus replied, 'The times and occasions are set by my father's own authority, and it is not for you to know when they will be.'[8]

So, during the lifetime of Jesus, some people, including some of his own friends, felt that the kingdom of God was an earthly kingdom. When this did not materialize another interpretation emerged, that the kingdom of God was to be the end of the world and the second coming of Jesus. As the kingdom was 'at hand' the expectation was that the world was going to end very soon, that Jesus would come a second time as a judge, and that people had to repent and believe in Jesus or be condemned to hell. This concept was particularly strong amongst the early Christian communities who believed that the second coming would come in their own lifetimes. But when members of these communities began to die before the Lord's coming, doubts began to be expressed. We read in St Paul's letter to the Thessalonians, 'Christ has died, Christ is risen, Christ will come again,'[9] a prayer, still recited by Christians today, that looks forward to the second coming of Christ. There are many Christians today who expect the second coming of Jesus and there have been instances in which Christian denominations have predicted the second coming and the end of the world with precise dates and signs; but these events have not happened. Peter had the same difficulty with his community over the second coming. 'They will mock you and ask you, "He promised to come didn't he? Where is he? Our fathers have already died, but everything is still the same since the creation of the world." '10 Peter goes on, 'Do not forget one thing, my dear friends! There is no difference in the Lord's sight between one day and a thousand years, to him the two are the same.'11 A later notion was that of millenarianism, an idea based on the Book of Revelation,12 which said that Christ will come first and rule the world for a thousand years, and only then will the world come to an end.

Somewhat later in the development of the early Christian understanding came the idea that the kingdom of heaven was a place where people go after their death. 'Blessed are you poor, for yours is the kingdom of God' was taken to mean that if you are poor, there is no need to worry because after your death you will go straight to heaven. The kingdom of God has also been identified with evangelization and the extension of the Church. Wherever people have been converted and the Church is established, there the kingdom of God is thought to have come. The kingdom of God has thus been identified with the institutional Church. A modern view is that the kingdom means a kingdom of peace, justice, righteousness and love; so that where there is peace, justice, righteousness and love, there also is the kingdom of God. So, the word 'kingdom' is a dynamic word, revealing the dynamic aspect of God ruling, God in action. Actually we can say that the 'kingdom of God' means 'God'.

What did Jesus mean when he said that the kingdom of God is 'at hand'? 'At hand' clearly means that it is close, that one can reach out and touch it. It implies that a person has only to stretch out his or her hand to be able to just pick it up, almost as one can just stretch out a hand to pick up a glass of water on a nearby table. The phrase 'at hand' has also been taken to mean that God is within us, or that God is amongst us, or that God is all around us. Each of these phrases are limited because if we say that God is within we can take this to mean that he is not outside, or if God is outside, all around us, then it might be taken to mean that he is not within. The one phrase that is inclusive is that 'God is everywhere'. God is outside us, God is within us, God is among us, and God is around us. We can say that the whole universe is in God. *We are all in the kingdom of God.* 'The kingdom of God is at hand' is a statement of an eternal truth. The kingdom of God is the dynamic aspect of God. It means that God is everywhere, God is among us, within us, and outside us, and we are all already in God. In saying that the kingdom of God is at hand, Jesus was announcing an eternal and universal truth. He was making a statement of fact; just as we can say that the sun rises in the east and see this as a statement of fact and a universal truth (at least in an empirical sense). The universal and eternal truth is that God is everywhere, God was everywhere and God will be everywhere.

In Mark's version, Jesus also said, 'the time is fulfilled', or 'the time has come to an end'. There are different types of time. There is biological time in which a person grows from childhood into old age; this is natural time, the time of the day, the time needed to cover distance and space. Then there is psy-

chological time, which is born out of the desire to become. It is
a distance between what one is psychologically or spiritually,
and what one wants to become in the future. Psychological
time began with the desire of the first human beings, Adam and
Eve, who in the story of the Garden of Eden wanted to become
like God. This desire created a gap between what they were
(not like God) and what they wanted to become (like God). It
was this desire that created both psychological time and the
means, that is, the eating of the fruit, by which they sought to
reach their goal. But actually there was no need for them to
become like God because they were already created in the
image and likeness of God and it was ignorance of this, forget-
ting this reality, that brought about their fall.

It is the desire to *become* that causes people to devise means
and ends; it is this desire that is the cause of human misery. It
is the desire to become that gives rise to religions and to the
identification of people as saviours. We can say that this is the
movement of time. Jesus was saying that this movement of time
came to an end when he realized that the kingdom of God was
at hand.

So how do we realize that the kingdom of God is at hand, or
that we are in God? The answer that Jesus gives is the one word
injunction, to 'repent'. Matthew's Gospel attaches importance
to the word 'repent'. The word is generally connected with sin
and conversion from sin, so that the injunction of Jesus is taken
to mean repent of your sins or 'convert' from your sins. The
word for repent in Hebrew is *shub*. The prophets used this word
when they asked people to come back to God, that is, to come
back to the law and to observe the law.

But as we shall see, Jesus was not calling the people to come
back to the law. Rather, he was calling people to see the eternal

truth that God is everywhere and that all people are in God. The Gospels were all written in Greek and the Greek word used for repentance is *metanoia*, which has the meaning of a radical change of mind. But *metanoia* also has a much more profound meaning. The word comes from Platonic philosophy in which reality is seen on four levels. The first is the body, the second is the individual soul, the third is the universal soul or *nous* and the fourth is One, or God. The word *meta* means to transcend or to go beyond. For example we can say that metaphysics is that which transcends physics or the physical world. So *metanoia* means to go beyond the *nous*. To find God each person has to transcend his or her identification with the body, with the individual soul, and even with the universal soul, and only then can the 'One', God or the kingdom of God, be found.

So if God is everywhere and to realize this all one has to do is to 'repent', if the meaning of repent is to somehow go beyond or transcend, how does one actually do this? It is important to realize that the word 'repent' does not imply a positive action, a movement towards a positive goal. Rather it implies a negative action. It is like the little fish in the ocean that does not know that it is in the ocean and is searching for the ocean. The little fish asks a big fish, 'Tell me, where is the ocean?' The big fish responds by saying, 'my dear little one, the ocean is everywhere. You are living and moving and have your being in it. You cannot live one minute without the ocean. Stop all your searching and realize that you are already in the ocean.' In the same way Jesus announced the eternal truth to humanity that God is like an infinite ocean and we are all like the little fish in the ocean searching for God. We cannot find God through movement, by going hither and thither. What we have to do is to stop all our movements and realize that we are already in God.

So the word 'repent' does not imply doing something positive, but rather it means that we should renounce all our doings, and stop all our movements. What Jesus is saying is that we cannot 'come' to God through movement, through a way, or through a path, but that it is only by renouncing all movements and ways, and all paths that we can find that we are already in God. The word 'repent' contains a simple and radical message, and that message is quite simply that the only way to find the kingdom of God is to stop the movement of time, end the movement of desire to become, and to renounce all ways to God. There is no *way* to God for God is everywhere.

The revolutionary message of Jesus is that ways and means, including religious observances, have a value in as much as they help one to come to that repentance, but to find the kingdom it is necessary to go beyond all ways. When Jesus was asked by the Pharisees when the kingdom of God was coming he said, 'The kingdom of God is not coming with signs to be observed! Nor will they say, "Lo, here it is!" or "There!" For behold the kingdom is in the midst of you.'[13]

Chapter 2

The experience of the kingdom of God

Jesus had to experience the good news of the kingdom of God in his own life before he could proclaim it. This experience took place at his baptism when the heavens opened and the Spirit of God came upon him and he discovered that he was the Son of God. This was the moment at which Jesus realized his true self and his relationship with the Father.

There are two aspects of this experience of the kingdom of God. The first can be described as a breakthrough in human consciousness, or as the entry of God's Spirit into the human heart. Through this the human being discovers that the kingdom of God is everywhere and that he or she is in the kingdom of God. The second aspect is the realization of one's identity in relationship to God. When the human consciousness of Jesus opened, the Spirit of God entered him and he realized that he was the Son of God. He did not *become* the Son of God, he had always been the Son of God and at that moment he became conscious of this fact. In this sense the kingdom experience is the coming of the Spirit into one's life and simultaneously one becomes aware of God's presence and discovers one's real identity in relationship to God.

The eternal reality of the kingdom of God became a present historical reality in Jesus. The kingdom of God lived, moved and acted in him. When the Pharisees accused him of casting out demons by the power of Beelzebub, the prince of demons, Jesus answered, 'But if it is by the Spirit of God that I cast out demons, then the kingdom of God has come.'[14] When Philip said to him, 'Lord show us the Father and we shall be satisfied,' Jesus replied:

> He who has seen me has seen the Father. Do you not believe that I am in the Father and the father is in me? The words I say to you I do not speak on my own authority but the Father who dwells in me does his work. Believe me that I am in the Father and the Father is in me, or else believe me for the sake of the works themselves.[15]

The discovery of the kingdom of God, the discovery of one's true identity, is experienced as a sudden event. Jesus describes this through a parable, 'the kingdom of God is like a man who found treasure in a field. He buried it again, went home, sold everything and bought the field.'[16] The parable can be taken to mean that a person who finds the kingdom of God has a similar experience to the man who found the treasure in the field. Just as he buried it happily, went home, sold everything and bought the field, so also the person who finds the kingdom of God will joyfully, spontaneously and choice-lessly give up all his or her possessions because what he or she has found is greater than that being given up. The truth is so clear that there is no time to think, no time to make choices.

The kingdom is also something that can be found as one searches for it. Again Jesus described this through a parable. He said that the kingdom of God is like a merchant in search of pearls. When he found the pearl of great value he went home, sold everything and bought that pearl.[17] Just as the merchant went home, sold everything happily and bought the pearl of great price, so also the person who finds the kingdom of God gives up everything joyfully because what he or she has found is greater that what is being lost. The choice is a choice-less choice. There is no time spent in thinking and evaluating. The truth is so clear that there is no choice to be made.

The discovery of the kingdom of God is not only sudden it is also unexpected. Jesus described this aspect through another parable. He said, 'The kingdom of God is like a net thrown into the sea. When the fishermen pulled the net to the shore, they divided the good fish and the bad fish. They took the good ones and threw away the bad ones.' And he went on to say, 'It will be like this at the end of the age. The angels will go out and gather up the evil people from among the good, and will throw them into the fiery furnace, where they will cry and grind their teeth.'[18]

To understand this parable it is necessary to look at the way in which the Gospel stories were compiled and written down. This parable seems to be unclear in its meaning for Jesus was certainly not speaking about good and bad people, nor was he speaking about the end of the world, or heaven and hell. He was speaking about the experience of the person who finds the kingdom of God. It is likely that the original parable was re-interpreted before it was written down and put in the context of the second coming, judgment and the end of the world. The original parable makes more sense when it is seen to be saying that the kingdom of God is like a net thrown into the sea, and that when the fishermen pulled it to the shore they found a very big fish. They joyfully took the big fish and threw away the small ones. Such an interpretation is found in the Gospel of Thomas. Just as the fishermen happily gave away the smaller fish for the sake of the big one, so too a person who finds the kingdom of God gives away the smaller things of life for the sake of the kingdom, because what he or she has found is greater than what is being lost. Again it is a choice-less choice.

All these parables about the kingdom of God tell us that something has to be given up for the sake of the kingdom. When we consider what is it that has to be given up it is important not to think of it in a materialistic sense. Jesus is not advocating external renunciation but internal renunciation, renouncing one's dependency on things that are passing and finding security in the eternal. For when one finds the kingdom of God one realizes that it is eternal and that the material things in which one normally finds security are transient and passing. The kingdom of God is infinite whereas that in which we normally place our trust is finite.

Jesus told his followers that to find the kingdom of heaven one has to give up the unreal self for the sake of the real self. He told them that the ego has to be renounced for the sake of God. It is renouncing the master-slave relationship with God for the parent-child relationship. It is renouncing the lower for the higher. Jesus asks for a positive renunciation in that one is gaining more than one is giving up. Negative renunciation would be renunciation of the things of this world for the hope of reward, either in this life, or after death. This distinction between positive and negative renunciation can be seen in the story of a king who one day went hunting in the forest.

> There was once a king who went hunting and he came across a beautiful young man taking care of the sheep. A mark on the face of the young man reminded the king of his lost son, who had been stolen and thought to have been killed when he was a tiny baby. So the king asked the young man who he was, whereupon the young man told him that he was the son of a shepherd

from a nearby village. The king wanted to make sure so he went to the village to ask the shepherd about the identity of this young man. At first the shepherd insisted that the young man was his real son. But when the king threatened him he admitted that he had found his son abandoned in the forest when he was a tiny baby. The king's baby had been taken by his enemies and left in the forest so that wild animals would kill him. But before this happened the shepherd came and found the baby, and as he had no children of his own, he joyfully took the child to his house thinking that he was a gift from God, and bought him up as his own son. Once the young man realized that he was not the son of the shepherd, but the son of a king he had no choice but to accept his real identity.

This is what happens when one finds oneself in the presence of God. A person who finds himself or herself in the presence of God realizes that he or she is the son or daughter of God but has been living like a son or daughter of the shepherd. Such a person has to renounce their identity as the son or daughter of a shepherd and accept their true identity as the son or daughter of God. When Jesus spoke of renunciation he was speaking of the renunciation of one's false identity for the sake of one's real identity.

At one level the experience of the kingdom of God is an individual experience but this individual experience then grows into a universal experience. It is an opening to the universal consciousness in which the whole of humanity, past, present and future, indeed the whole of creation, finds a place. Again Jesus described in a parable the way in which the individual experience of the kingdom of God grows into a universal experience, becoming open to the whole of humanity and creation:

> A man takes a mustard seed, the smallest seed in the world and plants it. It puts out such large branches that the birds come and make their nest in its shade.[19]

If the experience of the kingdom of God were to remain an individual experience then such a person could not be a saviour of humanity and creation, and could not have good news to proclaim. Just as a river at its source is a small stream and grows bigger as it moves towards the sea until it merges with it, so the individual search becomes universal, individual discovery becomes universal and individual salvation becomes universal. With the discovery of the kingdom of God one individual grows into the whole of creation.

The kingdom of God unfolds naturally and spontaneously. Once it is experienced all efforts have to be renounced. One has to remain silent, like the little fish in the sea looking for the ocean, and wait patiently for the kingdom to grow. Again Jesus described this unfolding through a parable of a man who scattered seed in his field:

> He sleeps at night, is up and about during the day, and all the while the seeds are sprouting and growing. Yet he does not know how it happens. The soil itself makes the plants grow and bear fruit; first the tender stalk appears, then the ear and finally the ear full of corn. When the corn is ripe, the man starts cutting it with his sickle because harvest time has come.[20]

The kingdom experience is an experience of creativity. Creativity does not come about through the effort of mind but when the mind relaxes and remains silent and effortless. In that virginal state of mind creativity manifests itself.

The experience of the kingdom of God is an experience of transformation and indwelling. Jesus describes this aspect of the kingdom through the parable of the yeast. 'The kingdom of heaven is like a woman who took yeast and put in three measures of meal until it was leavened.'[21] Just as the meal is leavened when the yeast is added so also a person is transformed by the experience of the kingdom. When the 'leaven' of the kingdom enters the 'meal' of a man or woman, the person becomes divine and the divine becomes human. God lives in the human being and the human being lives in God. It is a mutual indwelling and a mutual transformation.

The kingdom of God is an undivided whole and cannot be experienced in a divided way. It does not matter whether a man or woman discovers the kingdom at the beginning of their lives, in the middle or at the end. Each person has a complete discovery, for God cannot give himself or herself partially. God is an undivided whole and gives himself or herself fully. Jesus likened this aspect of the kingdom of God to a householder who went out early in the morning to hire laborers for his vineyard:

> After agreeing with the laborers a denarius a day he sent them into his vineyard. And going out about the third hour he saw others standing idle in the market place and to them he said, 'You go to into the vineyard too, and whatever is right I will give you.' So they went. Going out again about the sixth hour and the ninth hour, he did the same. And about the eleventh hour he went out and found others standing and he said to them, 'Why do you stand here idle all day?' They said to him, 'Because no-one has hired us.' He said to them, 'You go into the vineyard too.' And when those hired about the eleventh hour came, each of them received a denarius. Now when the first came they thought they would receive more but each of them also received a denarius. On receiving it they grumbled at the householder saying, 'These last worked only one hour, and you have made them equal to us, who have the burden of the day and the scorching heat.' But he replied to one of them, 'Friend, I am doing you no wrong. Did you not agree with me for a denarius? Take what belongs to you and go. Am I not allowed to do what I choose with what belongs to me? Or do you begrudge my generosity? So the last will be first and the first last.[22]

The expression 'the first will be last and the last will be first' should not be understood in the sense of elevating the lower and degrading the higher. It means that in the experience of the kingdom of God there are no grades, all are equal because God cannot give himself in degrees. People may experience God partially, but God always gives himself or herself fully and wholly.

The Good News of the kingdom can also be experienced as a threat. It can lead people who are not looking for it into a crisis that calls for an immediate decision. Jesus described this aspect of the experience of the kingdom of God in the parable of the rich man's steward who was dismissed for squandering his master's goods.

> And the steward said to himself, 'What shall I do since my master is taking the stewardship away from me? I am not strong enough to dig, and I am ashamed to beg. I have decided what to do so that people will receive me into their houses when I am no longer a steward.' Summoning his debtors one by one he said to the first, 'How much do you owe my master?' He replied, 'A hundred measures of oil.' Then he said to him, 'Take your bill, sit down quickly and write fifty.' Then to another, 'How much do you owe?' He replied, 'A hundred measures of wheat.' Then he said to him, 'Take your bill and write eighty.' The master commended the dishonest steward for his prudence.[23]

The rich man took away the steward's job without offering anything. The steward realized that he had lost his security and saw the need to act immediately. The experience of the kingdom of God challenges our security and in particular the security we have in our religious traditions and beliefs. The ministry of Jesus was to tell people that the law and the temple were not absolute and had only relative value. The experience of the kingdom of God puts those who have built their spiritual houses on the law and the temple into a crisis. The kingdom invites them into a higher relationship with God, but if people are not open to grow into this new relationship, if they are satisfied with the law and the temple, then the message of the kingdom can become a threat and the good news can become bad news.

Chapter 3

Humanity searches for God and God searches for humanity

A mother and her child once went to a crowded market and somehow became separated. The mother was searching for the child and the child was searching for her mother. Eventually they met and in the very same moment each one saw the other; the child shouted, 'Mummy,' in the same instant as the mother shouted, 'Andrea'. As soon as the mother found her child she knew that her child had been searching for her and as soon as the child found her mother she too knew that her mother had been searching for her. In our search for God, God is searching for us. When we find God, God finds us. The kingdom of God is the experience of finding God and being found by God.

An important aspect of the experience of the kingdom of God is the realization that Jesus is God who came to find lost humanity. In Jesus, God finds humanity and in Jesus humanity finds God. The Gospels make this aspect of finding very clear. From the human point of view the kingdom experience is like finding a hidden treasure such as a precious pearl or a big fish. Likewise Jesus talks of God searching for humanity in the parables of the lost sheep, the lost coin and the prodigal, or lost, son.

> What man of you, having a hundred sheep, if he has lost one of them does not leave the ninety-nine in the wilderness and go

after one which is lost, until he finds it. And when he has found it, he lays it on his shoulders rejoicing. And when he comes home, he calls together his friends and neighbors, saying to them, 'Rejoice with me, for I have found my sheep which was lost.' Just so, I tell you, there will be more joy in heaven over one sinner who repents than over ninety-nine righteous persons who need no repentance.[24]

This does not mean that there are 99 sheep that are not in need of repentance; rather it means that there is only one sheep, and that one sheep is the whole of the humanity that God has lost. He comes to find this one lost sheep.

In telling the story of the lost coin, Jesus said, 'What woman, having 10 silver coins, if she loses one coin does not light a lamp and sweep the house and seek diligently until she finds it? She calls together her friends and neighbors, saying, "Rejoice with me, for I have found the coin which I had lost." Just so I tell you there is joy before the angels of God over one sinner who repents.'[25] There is only one coin that is lost, and that coin is the whole of humanity. God came to find that coin, to find his lost humanity.

In the parable of the prodigal son we have a beautiful example of God finding humanity and humanity finding God. The prodigal son is the whole of humanity that has left God, but once the son discovered he could not find fulfillment outside God he came back to God.[26] The parable also makes it clear that it is not only the son who comes back to the father but that the father was waiting for the son. 'While he was yet at a distance, his father saw him and had compassion, and ran and embraced him and kissed him.' It is an encounter of the father finding the son and the son finding the father, the encounter of God finding humanity and of humanity finding God. The kingdom of God is an experience of God searching for and finding humanity and of humanity searching for and finding God. The story of Zacchaeus also illustrates God finding humanity and humanity finding God. Zacchaeus was the head of the tax collectors, in which role he is representative of the head of sinners or the head of the rejected. 'And now the tax collectors and the sinners were all drawing near to him; and the Pharisees and the scribes murmured saying, "This man receives sinners and eats with them."' [27] Perhaps Zacchaeus had heard about Jesus and his predilection for publicans and sinners. Perhaps he had thought of inviting Jesus to his house and of organizing a great feast, but he didn't have the courage to invite a man of God into the house of a sinner. Perhaps Zacchaeus wanted to tell Jesus that being the head of the tax collectors was not a very easy job. Perhaps he wanted to say that he did not want to do what he had been doing but that he had been forced into this situation. Perhaps he was not as secure as the Scribes and the Pharisees who were able to invite Jesus whenever they wanted to.

Zacchaeus was profoundly attracted to the person of Jesus but was not sure whether Jesus would accept his invitation. Psychologically we can say that he was attracted to that which corresponded to all that he had repressed inside himself. The Scribes and the Pharisees, the so-called spiritual people, repress negative sentiments in the name of the ideal of righteousness, whereas sinners repress good sentiments. Saints fight with the devil, the evil, whilst sinners fight with the angels, with the good. In fact Jesus was neither 'righteous' according the Law like the Pharisees, nor a sinner like Zacchaeus. He transcended all categories of righteous and unrighteous. He was full of compassion for sinners and was angry with the Scribes and the

Pharisees, and it was this that made Zacchaeus search for him. In Jesus he had found someone to whom he could open himself up and have a dialog. Interestingly Zacchaeus was very short in stature. This represents inferiority, aspects of him that had not grown and which looked for attention, acceptance, recognition, love and compassion. The Scribes and the Pharisees, on the other hand, felt more at ease with the tax collectors and the sinners than with Jesus because they felt morally superior. Jesus did not attract the righteous because he showed up the relativity of their righteousness.

Sinners could not feel secure in front of the Scribes and the Pharisees because they did not follow the law, but they could find security with Jesus. The publicans and sinners moved closer to Jesus because he transcended the so-called just and unjust. According to Jesus neither the just nor the unjust had discovered the infinite treasure hidden in their hearts and they both needed self-discovery. They had not yet discovered the treasure hidden in the field or the pearl of great value. Both were called to give up their acquired superficial virtues or vices and to enter their profound being; there they would discover true and eternal righteousness. This is a free gift of God which cannot be acquired by human hand, and which cannot be stolen.

It is difficult for the so-called 'just' to respond to this call of Jesus because it implies leaving their foundation, which they have constructed on the justice of the law. It means realizing that justice that comes from the law is relative; it has no eternal foundation. It means accepting the relativity of the law and of the temple. Although it was difficult for the Scribes and the Pharisees to respond to the call of Jesus, such a response was easy for the 'sinners' because their only security is their insecurity, their inferiority. Their unrighteousness is their benediction. People who do not have security based on the law are more open to respond to the call of God.

Zacchaeus was a rich and important person, the head of the publicans. But he was looking for love, attention and acceptance and was too timid to encounter Jesus directly. He just wanted to see Jesus first, so he did something quite extraordinary, he climbed a sycamore tree. However, it appears that Jesus knew him already for he called him by name. Perhaps he had heard about Zacchaeus and wanted to see the head of the sinners.

There was a great attraction between the head of the 'saints' and the head of the 'sinners'. Zacchaeus' love for Jesus was so great that this great love received a response of great love. 'Zacchaeus, make haste and come down for I must stay at your house today.' Jesus does not only see the straight road of the Pharisees but lifts up his eyes to look above and see above if anybody is waiting for him there. The story is just like the parable of the prodigal son. In this the son was returning to the father, but the father saw his son while he was far away and ran to him. Before Zacchaeus could say anything Jesus called him by name and offered himself as his guest. Jesus did not say, 'You are a sinner and you need repentance,' he just invited himself to Zacchaeus' house.

And so a miracle happened. Unconditional love transforms negative energy, the energy that accumulated material riches, into positive energy that shared material riches with others. Zacchaeus' identity was built around the accumulation of material wealth by wrongful means, just as the identity of the Scribes and the Pharisees was built on the accumulation of spiritual wealth by adhering to the Law. Zacchaeus had no moral or spiritual security, for he was considered a sinner, and the accumulation of material wealth or intellectual wealth failed to give him real security. This sort of wealth creates a desire for people to preserve everything they have accumulated; they are afraid of losing it and want to protect it.

Materialism not only applies to the accumulation of material wealth but also to the accumulation of spiritual virtues. Just as the materially rich try to protect their material wealth, so the spiritually rich try to protect their spiritual wealth, their so-called virtues. However, everything that is acquired is artificial and does not belong to the essence of our being. Only unconditional love can free one from these accumulations and release energy that flows out freely in sharing, without desire for rewards and without fear of loss.

Real security is our 'being' which is a free gift of God. Nobody can rob us of our 'being' and only in our 'being' can we have authentic security. This is the treasure lost sight of by humanity but which remains hidden in the human heart. When we forget our 'being,' we move away from God. Jesus came to search for and to find the 'being' that humanity had lost. An action that comes from our 'being' is an action of unconditional love and it transforms and liberates. Actions that come from our identification with material, intellectual or spiritual accumulations have the quality of imprisoning. Jesus had discovered his 'being' and so his words and actions came from his 'being', the Father, and so had the quality of trans-forming.

Only an action of unconditional love can awaken in a person like Zaccheus the hidden treasure of the kingdom of God. The unconditional love of God transformed the energy of Zaccheus, who had been accumulating material wealth by wrong means, into an energy in which he shared his material accumulations in an extraordinary way. He said, 'Behold Lord, the half of my goods I give to the poor and if I have defrauded anyone of anything, I restore it fourfold.' Jesus did not demand anything but only said, 'Today I must stay at your house… today salvation has come to this house, for he is also the son of Abraham, and the son of man came to seek and to save the lost.'[28]

Zacchaeus is our rejected self, the self that has moved from God but which is longing for God. We can also say that Jesus is God who came to search for and find what was lost. For God, humanity is lost; for humanity, God is lost. Jesus and Zacchaeus represent the beautiful meeting of God and humanity. This is the gospel: Jesus is God who comes in search of humanity and finds it – Jesus is a human being searching for God and finding him. God receives his prodigal son or daughter, and the prodigal son, or daughter, returns to the father. Humanity returns to God and God finds humanity.

When Jesus said, 'The Son of Man in fact has come to search and save those who are lost,' we should not think that there were some who were lost and there were others who were not lost, some who were in need of conversion and others who were not in need of conversion. The whole of humanity is lost: not only has humanity lost God but God has also lost humanity. Humanity lost its 'being', the kingdom of God, the hidden treasure, and Jesus came to search for and find this hidden treasure on behalf of humanity. He came to search for and find humanity on behalf of God.

Jesus sets the 'righteousness' of the Pharisees in the context of the 'unrighteousness' of Zacchaeus. In doing so he offers us the possibility of our seeing the law and the temple in the light of his gospel of new life. The law is a great ideal. It is a gift of

God to humanity and it reveals the will of God to humanity. However ideals are like idols or statues – they do not change, whereas life requires changes to be made in response to different situations and times. The law reveals a great ideal, it tells us what is right and wrong and it divides people into righteous and unrighteous. But the law does not help us to be right in daily life situations that demand flexibility and change as we grow, and at the level of the law there is no solution for the moral and spiritual problems of humanity. It is only when a person transcends this level that he or she can understand the eternal plan of God and open the door for all humanity, both the just and the unjust.

Jesus manifests a new level of consciousness, the consciousness of the kingdom of God according to which both the just and the unjust need conversion, need to discover their eternal being. For the secure and rich the call of Jesus, the message of Jesus, is a threat, because the gospel demands that they leave the security of their spiritual house and begin to walk on the way of eternal life. Such people have to find some excuse to reject the message of Jesus. To them Jesus said:

> To what then shall I compare the men of this generation and what are they like? They are like children sitting in the market place and calling to one another, 'we piped for you, and you did not dance, we wailed and you did not weep.' For John the Baptist has come eating no bread and drinking no wine and you say, 'He has a demon.' The son of man has come eating and drinking and you say, 'Behold a glutton and a drunkard, a friend of tax collectors and sinners!' Yet wisdom is justified by all her children.[29]

Just as one group played the wedding dance and the other group did not dance, and just as one group of children sang the funeral song and the other group did not mourn, in the same way Jesus shared his experience of the kingdom of God, but some people will always find an excuse for not joining in. As the tax collectors and sinners received baptism from John the Baptist, the Pharisees, the teachers of the Law, suggested that as he did not eat bread and did not drink wine, he must have been possessed by a demon. But when they saw that Jesus did eat bread and drink wine they rejected him and his message, proclaiming that he was a glutton and a drunkard, a friend of the tax collectors and other outcasts. Those who do not want to hear the message of the kingdom of God will always find an excuse.

The words that Jesus spoke two thousand years ago are valid today and for all time. When the truth, which is eternal life, comes, it will find two types of people. It will find the poor, the hungry, and the insecure living outside the house and excommunicated, and it will find the rich and the satisfied living secure and inside the house. Eternal life loves them both for it transcends both. Men and women in the first group are blessed, because without security it is easier for them to enter new life, the way. Those in the second group are in danger because, having security, they have the option of rejecting the gospel and life.

Eternal life is not a choice made once and for all, but at each moment of one's life; eternal life is always an interior journey, to leave the psychological past and to enter the eternity of the psychological present. The one gift we can give to others is to not build a spiritual house and stop our interior journey. We must always be on the journey. We must always follow eternal life, which reveals and transcends. The person on the journey has no time to judge others. The journey becomes the message.

Only those who have constructed houses on the way and who have stopped their journey indulge in the luxury of discussing their houses, comparing them with other houses and defending them against others. The person on the way has nothing to defend, nothing to compare with what others have, and, leaving everything behind that they possess or have experienced, they remain poor, without a house. As Jesus said, 'The foxes have their holes, the birds have their nests, but the Son of Man has nowhere to lay his head.'[30] This should not be seen only as an external experience, but also as the internal experience of one who is the way, the truth and the life.

Jesus discovered the infinite treasure of the kingdom of God and announced this good news to humanity. But not all were enthusiastic; many were against him and rejected his message. In the Beatitudes Jesus tells us for whom it is easy to find this infinite treasure of the Kingdom of God.

Part **2**

The Beatitudes – the personal experience of Jesus

Is it only?
Is it only when we don't know you
that we know you?
Is it only when we lose you
that we find you forever?
Is it only when we feel your absence
that we are close to you?
Is it only when we are going away from you
that we are coming very near to you?
Is it only when we are in crisis
that we discover you?
Is it only when we enter into darkness
that we find you, the true light?
Is it only when we are unable to pray
that we discover true prayer?
Is it only when we hate you
that we begin to love you?
Is it only when we misunderstand you
that we begin to understand you?
Is it only when we are unable to speak to you
that we learn to speak with you?
Is it only when we suffer
that we realize your love for us?
Is it only when we disobey you
that we learn how to obey you truly?
O God is the world losing you
only to find you forever?
Are you losing this world
only to find it forever?

4

Blessed are the poor

'Blessed are the poor in spirit for theirs is the kingdom of heaven,' says the Gospel of Matthew. 'Blessed are you poor for yours is the kingdom of God,' says the Gospel of Luke. The kingdom of God is the dynamic aspect of God, the infinite treasure hidden in the heart of every human being and every creature. Jesus was saying that those who are poor materially and spiritually are blessed because it is easier for them to find this treasure.

The greatness and simplicity of holy people is such that each word they utter contains the whole truth. If we understand a single Beatitude we can understand all the other Beatitudes for each is complete in itself; each communicates the same message but in a different way.

Imagine a road running through a forest. At one point in the road there was a huge tree and on one of the branches there was a bundle containing precious diamonds that had been hidden. One day heavy rain created a big pit under the tree and a traveller walking on the road accidentally fell into it. He could neither look forward nor look back, so he looked up and saw the bundle in the branches of the tree, climbed the tree and, to his immense surprise, discovered the cache of precious treasure.

The tree is the tree of eternity, and the road is the road of time, the movement of the past into the future. The tree of eternity is present everywhere but people follow the path of time in their attempt to reach eternity. However, the path of time, the road, cannot take you to the treasure of eternity. Only those who fall into the pit, who fail on the road of time, are blessed because it is easy for them to find the treasure of eternity.

Jesus came to announce the gospel of life and to invite people to eternal life. To enter eternal life is to repent, to renounce, and to die to one's ego. Without the death of the false 'I' and the emergence of the real 'I' there can be no eternal life. To enter into eternal life one has to be 'born from above', that is, born of the spirit. Jesus told Nicodemus, 'I am telling you the truth: no one can see the kingdom of God unless he is born again.'[31] To find the kingdom of God is to discover the meaning and purpose of one's existence and the meaning of death. Only those who face death know what it means and only then can they find the meaning of life.

Jesus' call to the kingdom of God is an invitation to life, and he saw that some will accept the gospel, and others will reject it. The people who followed Jesus accepted the gospel; they were simple people, sinners and tax collectors, poor both materially and spiritually. These were people who did not have a secure spiritual 'house'. They were the poor in spirit. On the other hand the people who rejected Jesus were those who had spiritual security. Jesus realized that the poor were blessed because they were better able to enter life, to begin this new life. The rich people, those inside the house of spiritual security, had less opportunity precisely because they had found security in the house, and this is death.

What Jesus was saying was, 'Blessed are you who are poor, insecure and hungry because it is easy for you to enter life, to begin the journey, because you are already outside the house, on the road.' To the rich he was saying, 'How pitiable is your situation, you have security but your security is your death. Your house is your tomb.' This is not a condemnation, rather is it an expression of love and compassion expressed in a negative way. The Beatitudes and their opposites, the 'woes', are two sides of the same coin of love; love that does not get angry is not love.

The materially poor are those who have only food for today; they do not know what will happen tomorrow. Their work brings them only enough money to buy food for today and in this sense death is a daily reality for them. The materially poor have no future and cannot imagine one, they can only ask for their daily bread. Since death is a daily reality for the poor, and since death is the ultimate and inevitable destiny of our human existence, they are much closer to asking such fundamental questions about the meaning of life and death. Once they have found the meaning of life and death, their daily lives and struggles will have a deeper meaning. However this material poverty can also make a person angry for when he compares himself with the rich and blames them for his poverty, he may take up violent struggle against them.

Material riches cannot save one from death. Death has to be faced by everyone individually. Since the poor face death each moment of their life it is easier for them to find eternal life, the kingdom of God, which alone gives meaning and fulfillment to their lives. Materially rich people believe that their tomorrow is guaranteed, they do not face death each moment of their life and for them death is something that happens sometime in the future. But all their material wealth cannot protect them from the inevitability of death. Jesus exhorted his listeners not to trust so much in their riches. Once a man in the crowd said to

Jesus, 'Teacher, tell my brother to divide the property our father left us.' Jesus answered him, 'My friend, who gave me the right to judge or to divide the property between you two... watch out and guard yourselves from every type of greed, because a person's true life is not made up of things he owns, no matter how rich he may be.' Then Jesus told them a parable about people who accumulate riches for themselves:

> There was once a rich man who had land which bore good crops. He began to think to himself, 'I haven't anywhere to keep all my crops. What can I do? This is what I will do. I will tear down my barns and build bigger ones where I will store my corn and all my other goods. Then I will say to myself, "Lucky Man! You have all the good things you need for many years. Take life easy, eat, drink and enjoy yourself!" ' But God said to him, 'You fool! This very night you will have to give up your life, so then who will get all those things you have kept for yourself?' This is how it is with those who pile up riches for themselves but are not rich in God's sight.[32]

People who are materially rich but who do not place their trust in those riches can also be rich in the sight of God. Material wealth is necessary for human existence and there is not necessarily any danger in accumulating it; one needs to work to acquire it. But if one trusts in material wealth and identifies with it, one is not rich in the sight of God. Jesus exhorts his disciples to seek eternal riches that can never decrease because 'no thief can get to them and no moth can destroy them.'[33]

Another story is that of a rich young man who had the desire for eternal life. He observed all the commandments sincerely but Jesus told him, 'There is still one more thing you need to do. Sell all you have and give the money to the poor and you will have riches in heaven, then come and follow me.'[34] The young man was then sad because he was rich and identified himself with and had security in his riches, without which he had no existence. In reality his riches were not an essential part of his being for he could not take them with him at his death. His security was actually his 'death' for he was not able to follow a 'way' of life. He was sad, for with his burden of artificial riches he could not enter the kingdom of God. The door to the kingdom is narrow, not in a physical sense, but in the sense that only the essential aspect of our being goes through it; all acquired things have to be left behind.

The kingdom of God with its eternal riches is the essential nature of all human beings made in the image and likeness of God. This treasure can neither increase nor decrease. No thief can reach it and no moth can destroy it. It is easier for those who are poor in acquired riches to find their essential riches, the kingdom of God. When Jesus called people to follow him it was poor fishermen who responded easily:

> As Jesus walked along the shore of Lake Galilee he saw two fishermen, Simon and his brother Andrew, catching fish with a net. Jesus said to them, 'Come with me and I will teach you to catch men.' At once they left their nets and went with him. He went a little further on and saw two other brothers, James and John, the sons of Zebedee. They were in their boat getting their nets ready. As soon as Jesus saw them, he called them; they left their father Zebedee in the boat with the hired men and went with Jesus.[35]

The human mind always seeks security, which can be material security, intellectual security or spiritual security. On the material level there is some justification for needing security, to have a house and a job and to have a family. But the human mind extends the need for this security to intellectual and spiritual levels and this creates problems, because in eternal life one cannot seek security, one has to let it go.

God called Abraham and asked him to leave everything and go to the place, which he would show him. Abraham was already on the journey without knowing his destination. He did not build a solid house on the way but lived in tents. A tent is a temporary house and it is easy to move it somewhere else whenever one wants. A person who constructs a solid house with stone foundations stops his or her journey and becomes a watchman, a guardian of the house. He or she begins to collect things for the house, inside and outside, and finds security in them. This can be true in the sense of an intellectual 'house' or a spiritual 'house' as much as a material house.

In the name of security one chooses death, for although there is security in houses and possessions, there is no life, there is no journey, life has stopped. There is only death. Eternal life, on the other hand, is an unending interior journey. Eternal life is not an unending continuity of the past, but is an unending journey from eternity to eternity. The spiritual journey is a journey from the security of the past into the eternity of the present, from the known into the unknown. There is always a danger that the human mind might abandon the spiritual journey and settle down in an intellectual or spiritual house, a tower of Babel, in which to forget the journey. This is spiritual death.

To be poor in spirit is not identifying with spiritual qualities. People can become rich by striving for spiritual qualities and holiness through their own efforts. Then they find security in these 'acquired' virtues. Just as people work very hard and accumulate material wealth and find security so also people strive very hard for spiritual wealth and security. Such spiritually rich people have security for the future and feel able to defend themselves on the day of judgment by showing all the good things they have done. However, all this is artificial and does not belong to the natural order; it needs to be protected and defended.

The poor in spirit are those who have *no* security in acquired spiritual wealth and who do *not* identify themselves with their virtues. They identify themselves with their original self, which is the image and likeness of God. This original self is naked and empty. Just as in death one leaves everything behind so also in spiritual death one has to give up all 'qualities' and find one's original state, which is to enter the kingdom of God. If anyone wants to enter the kingdom of God he or she has to be spiritually poor. Jesus said that people who try to preserve their false self will lose it, but those who renounce it will find their true self.

> If anyone wants to come with me he must forget self, take up his cross every day, and follow me. For whoever wants to save his own life will lose it, but whoever loses his life for my sake will save it. Will a person gain anything if he wins the whole world but is himself lost or defeated?[36]

Jesus called people to follow him and only those who are poor, who are not attached to their acquired wealth on any level of human existence, can follow him. As they went on their way, a man said to Jesus, 'I will follow you wherever you go.' Jesus said to him, 'Foxes have holes and birds have nests but the Son of Man has nowhere to lie down and rest.'[37] Jesus is life, and life is movement. Life cannot settle down in a hole or a nest. It is always on the move. Those who follow Jesus must be followers of the way, the life and the truth. Jesus said to another man, 'Follow me,' but the man replied, 'First let me go back and bury my father.'[38] This man was not free; he was attached emotionally. In that sense he was not poor but rich, and Jesus answered him, 'Leave the dead to bury their own dead, but as for you, go and proclaim the kingdom of God.'[39] Parents represent the past. Jesus invites people to leave the psychological past and to enter the eternity of the psychological present. People who are attached to their psychological past are not free to respond to the kingdom of God. The past is dead and the present cannot be involved with the past. Let the past bury the past. You live in the present, you live in the kingdom.

If one wants to see the kingdom here and now one must be free from the psychological past, otherwise one will project the past into the present, and the present then will be contaminated by the past. Such a person does not see what *is* but sees what *was*. Life is a series of 'presents' and the only reality is the 'present'. To live the life of the kingdom one has to be free from the psychological past and the psychological future. This does not mean freedom from the material or functional past or the functional future, as these are necessary for day-to-day living.

Of course it is difficult to free ourselves from the psychological past. We want to bury it, we want to do something about it and so we have psychoanalysis. The dead are in the cemetery and one can do two things in cemeteries. One can bury the dead or dig up the bones of the dead. So long as we are in the cemetery we are not in the village, in life. Jesus said, 'Let the dead bury their own dead,' that is, let the past bury the past, you come and live in the present. Another man said to Jesus, 'I will follow you sir, but first let me go and say good-bye to my family.' Jesus said to him, 'Anyone who starts to plow and then keeps looking back is of no use to the kingdom of God.'[40] If one starts plowing one has to concentrate on the present; and in life if one looks backwards or looks forward to the future, the pres-

ent is neglected and is not lived. A radical detachment from
the psychological past is necessary if one is to follow the way of
the kingdom, because the kingdom of God is in the present, in
the now. Jesus was very clear about this need to be detached
from the past.

Some people came to Jesus and asked him, 'Why is it that the
disciples of John the Baptist and the Pharisees fast, but yours do
not?' Jesus answered, 'Do you expect the guests at a wedding
party to go without food? Of course not! As long as the bridegroom is with them, they will not do that.'⁴¹

Fasting implies movement of time – to sacrifice something
today to get something tomorrow. Fasting always implies the
process of becoming, to sacrifice today for the sake of tomorrow.
However in the life of the kingdom of God there is no tomorrow, only today, only now. This now is meant to be joyful.
Today is meant for today and not as a means for tomorrow.
There is no psychological tomorrow although there will of
course be a functional tomorrow and a material tomorrow. The
statement, 'But the day will come when the bridegroom will be
taken away from them and they will fast,'⁴² might have been a
later addition. Jesus also used the example of old and new cloth
and old and new wineskins:

No one uses a piece of new cloth to patch up an old coat,
because the new patch will shrink and tear off some of the old
cloth, making a bigger hole. Nor does anyone put new wine into
used wineskins because the wine will burst the skins, and both
the wine and the skins will be ruined. Instead new wine must be
poured into fresh wineskins.⁴³

The way of Jesus is the way to eternity, the way of the now, the
way of today, the way of feasting, the way of new cloth, the way
of new wine, and the way of *unfolding* what is already there

within us. The way of the Pharisees is the way of time, the way of tomorrow, the way of fasting, the way of old cloth, the way of old wineskins, and the way of *becoming*. They belong to a different order and no one can put them together. New wine belongs to new wineskins. Those who are attached to old cloth and old wineskins cannot follow the way of the kingdom.

The story of Levi the tax collector is a story about a man who was materially rich but spiritually poor. Levi was considered to be a sinner and an outcast and when Jesus called him he 'got up and followed him.'[44] Jesus then had a meal in Levi's house. A large number of tax collectors and other outcasts were following him and many of them joined him and his disciples at the table. Some Pharisees, teachers of the Law, saw that Jesus was eating with these outcasts and tax collectors, so they asked his disciples, 'Why does he eat with such people?' Jesus heard them and answered, 'People who are well do not need a doctor, but only those who are sick. I have not come to call the righteous but the sinners.'[45] According to Jesus both were sick from the point of view of the kingdom of God. The tax collectors were sick because of their unrighteousness just as the Scribes and the Pharisees were sick because of their self-righteousness. The kingdom of God transcends both unrighteousness and self-righteousness. There is an irony in Jesus' statement, 'I have not come to call the righteous but sinners,' for the Pharisees were in sin but they were not aware of it. They were in great danger. The unrighteous outcasts and tax collectors were aware of their sin and so were in a better position to respond to the call of God. This call is not a conversion to legal righteousness that comes from observation of the law, but conversion to the righteousness of the kingdom of God, which transcends legal righteousness and legal unrighteousness. Jesus said, 'Unless your righteousness transcends that of the scribes and the Pharisees, you cannot enter the kingdom of God.' In the story of Jesus eating with Simon the Pharisee, there was a woman who lived a 'sinful' life and when she heard that Jesus was eating at the Pharisee's house she brought an alabaster jar full of perfume, stood behind Jesus, kissed his feet and poured the perfume onto them. When Simon saw this he said to himself, 'If this man were really a prophet he would know who this woman is who is touching him, he would know what kind of a sinful life she lives.'[46] Simon the Pharisee was rich spiritually. He had acquired virtues by observing the law. The woman was spiritually poor and was considered to be a great sinner. However, she knew her situation, she longed for love, she longed for compassion and she was attracted to Jesus just as Zacchaeus was attracted to him. Her longing and courage bore fruit for she received acceptance, compassion and love. Her life was transformed.

Simon the Pharisee, with his spiritual riches, thought that Jesus was spiritually rich and was his equal and so felt able to invite him to dinner. His spiritual riches made him look down on others. Actually Jesus was spiritually rich but his spiritual wealth was not acquired. It belonged to the essence of his being, the eternal riches of the kingdom of God. Rather than losing the riches of their essential being, sinners who came into contact with the kingdom of God were transformed into lovers of the kingdom. Simon the Pharisee's riches were artificial so he had to protect them all the time by keeping aloof from sinners and tax collectors. His clothes would be soiled, he did not need compassion, he did not need acceptance, and he did not need forgiveness. Simon was self-righteous. He was far from the kingdom of God.

Chapter 5

Spiritual and intellectual poverty

People who have intellectual systems about God are not spiritually poor and even people who belong to a religion are not poor in that religion itself makes them rich. A person who says, 'I am a Christian' or 'I am a Hindu' is not poor because he or she has a religion. If someone says 'I am a Buddhist' such a person is not poor because he or she has something to hold on to. If someone says, 'I am a Muslim' such a person is not poor because he or she has Islam. To be spiritually poor one has to be naked, empty, without any clothes, without a label. To be spiritually poor means to renounce all artificial clothing, everything acquired from outside and to be in one's original state. For to be naked is our original state. Those who are poor in this sense are blessed because theirs is the kingdom of God.

The kingdom of God is the way, the truth and the life. Jesus is the way, the truth and the life. It is a 'way', but *the* way is not a road, but truth itself. Truth is not a definition but life itself, and life is not static, but always moving. Truth cannot be defined because every definition of the truth is like a tomb and only the dead are put in tombs. Life is the way, a journey, a dynamic process, a movement towards the destiny of every person, a destiny in which our temporal state finds its final consummation with God. A man came to Jesus saying, 'I will follow you wherever you go,' and Jesus said to him, 'Foxes have their holes and birds have their nests, but the Son of Man has nowhere to lie down and rest.'[47]

Human life is like a river that runs towards the ocean to die to itself and become one with the ocean. In the same way human life is created to run towards God, to encounter its final death and to become one with God. Jesus is the life, the river, which flows towards the ocean. This river invites everyone who has built a house and settled on its bank to join it and not to forget life. Those who have no house on the bank, who are not settled in the religion of the law, are poor and are blessed because it is easy for them to respond to the call of the river and to follow her towards the sea. Every religion can be the house, the hole, and the nest in which people take shelter and forget about the river, life itself. Jesus explained this in the parable of the Pharisee and the tax collector who went to the temple to pray,

> The Pharisee stood apart by himself and prayed, 'I thank you, God, that I am not like that tax collector over there. I fast two days a week, and I give you a tenth of all my income.' The tax collector stood at a distance and would not even raise his face to heaven, but beat on his breast and said, 'God have pity on me a sinner,' Jesus concluded the parable by saying, 'I tell you, the tax collector, and not the Pharisee, was in the right with God when he went home.'[48]

The Pharisee identified himself with his spiritual virtues, which made him rich and secure, and he looked down on the tax collector. The Pharisee was satisfied with his riches, although he could not take them with him into the next world, and they could be lost at any time if he stopped practising his virtues. On the other hand, the tax collector had no acquired spiritual riches;

he had only vices and this made him surrender to God's mercy. He was much closer to finding the eternal and natural riches that come from God.

Blessed are those who are poor in acquired virtues for theirs is the kingdom of God. How pitiable will be the situation of those who identify themselves with their acquired virtues for it will be difficult for them to find the real virtue of the kingdom of God.

Many people seek the kingdom of God through a means or through a way. However, just as eternity cannot be reached through time, the kingdom of God cannot be reached through ways or means, for the kingdom, which is eternity, is not at the end of time. 'Way' implies distance, distance implies time, time implies effort and effort implies acquisition. Eternity cannot be acquired through effort and cannot be reached through time. This desire for eternity creates the ego, the ego creates the goal and hence the means, time and effort. It is desire that makes one spiritually rich, it is desire that creates the duality of the seeker and that which is sought, it is desire that creates time and it is desire that creates means and ways.

To be spiritually poor is to be without desire, to be empty, to be naked. To be spiritually poor is to be without a goal, to be without a means and to be without a way. In that emptiness and nakedness one discovers the kingdom of God as one's essential nature. This is something that no person can take away from another and nor give to another.

In the story of the Garden of Eden, humanity fell from the original state of holiness because of a desire to become 'better' than its original and God-intended state of wholeness. This was the desire to 'become' like God. But God created human beings in his own image and he did not create humanity to 'become' anything. In Adam and Eve humanity was forbidden to eat the fruit of *becoming*. The serpent told Adam and Eve that if they ate the fruit they would become like God, but the moment they ate the fruit of *becoming* they died spiritually; they fell from their true nature. If Eve had answered, 'We are already in the image and likeness of God and so there is no need to become like him,' the consequences would have been different. But she forgot and so created duality. So Adam and Eve were saying, 'I am not like God, I want to become like God, and the "way" of achieving this is to eat the fruit.'

The story of the Garden of Eden is about desire creating goals, means and effort. To be poor in spirit is to be free of desire including the desire to become like God. All the means and ways, that is, all religions, have value only if they make a person realize that means cannot bring one to God and that one is already in God. Acquired things in themselves are not bad for one needs to acquire things in life, but the problem is in identifying oneself with them, in making oneself rich, materially or spiritually. In a material sense one needs a house, a job, a family, but it is identifying with these things that makes one 'rich', and makes one forget one's original state. This takes one away from the kingdom of God.

Jesus said, 'How I pity you who are rich, you have had your fill.'[49] He realized that rich people find it difficult to respond to his call to eternal life because they have placed their security in their riches and have settled down in them. He illustrated this in the parable of the rich man who prepared a great feast and then sent his servants to summon the guests:

> But they all began, one after the other, to make excuses. The first one told the servant, 'I have bought a field and must go and look at it. Please accept my apologies.' Another one said, 'I have

bought five pairs of oxen and am on my way to try them out, please accept my apologies.' Another one said, 'I have just married and for that reason I cannot come.' The servant went back and told all this to his master who was furious and told his servant, 'Hurry out to the streets and alleys of the town and bring back the poor, the crippled the blind and the lame. Go out to the country roads and lanes and make people come in so that my house may be full. I tell you that none of those men who were invited will taste my dinner.'[50]

Jesus had discovered the infinite riches of the kingdom of God, and was inviting everyone to partake in this feast of the kingdom. However, people were too busy with their affairs to go to the banquet of the kingdom of God. Only the sinners, the tax collectors and prostitutes, the rejected in society, responded to the call to the feast of the kingdom of God. Jesus makes this point when he told the chief priests and the elders of the Jewish people the story of the vineyard owner who had two sons:

He went to the elder one and said, 'Son, go and work in the vineyard today.' 'I don't want to,' he answered, but he later changed his mind and went to the vineyard. Then the father went to the other son and said the same thing. 'Yes Sir,' he answered, but he did not go. Which of the two did what his father wanted?' 'The elder one,' they answered. So Jesus said to them, 'I tell you, the tax collectors and prostitutes are going into the kingdom of God ahead of you. For John the Baptist came to you showing you the right path to take, and you would not believe him. But the tax collectors and the prostitutes believed him. Even when you saw this, you did not later change your minds and believe him.[51]

Jesus realized that those who do not have intellectual or spiritual wealth are blessed and more able to find that natural state which is the kingdom of God. He realized that it was less easy for the materially, spiritually or intellectually rich for they take security from their wealth. When Jesus said, 'It is easier for a camel to go through the eye of a needle than for a rich man to enter the kingdom,'[52] he was not speaking about rich people going to hell, but about how one can enter the life of the kingdom in the here and now. The door to eternity, the door to the kingdom, is everywhere, or rather there is no door at all. This 'door-less' door is narrow, not in the sense of space and time, but in the sense that to enter the natural state one has to leave everything behind and pass through it, as one does at the moment of death. Jesus said, 'Unless a grain of wheat falls into the ground and dies, it remains alone, but when it dies it gives a mighty harvest.'

Jesus also said, 'Unless one renounces his father, mother, wife, husband and children one cannot enter the kingdom of heaven.'[53] A father and mother have to renounce even their children in the sense that children are for God and should not be a means to fulfill the ambitions of the parents. Children have to renounce their parents in that they are not there to fulfill their parents' ambitions, they are not there to provide continuity for their parents but they are meant for God. A husband has to renounce his wife in that his wife is for God and a wife has to renounce her husband in that her husband is not a means for her to fulfill her ambitions and desire, but rather her husband is meant for God. In this sense everyone becomes a unique manifestation of God and not a repetition of the past.

The Old Testament gives us the beautiful story of Abraham, a story that reveals the eternal truth of renunciation. Abraham did not want to die without a son, unable to continue his line. He asked God to give him a son and miraculously God gave him what he wanted. God then asked Abraham to sacrifice Isaac, his hope for continuity, because he saw that Abraham wanted this son for himself and not for God. He saw that Isaac had no individuality of his own, but was there just to continue his father's line. By thinking of Isaac in this way Abraham had already 'killed' his son, so he had to sacrifice his desire for continuity. Once he had done this he gave life back to Isaac who was thereby chosen for God.

In renouncing his continuity by offering Isaac, Abraham became free and lived in eternity and Isaac also became free from continuity and lived for eternity. In this story we see that the renunciation of desire for continuity means that that every person is chosen for God, for eternity.

As well as spiritual poverty, there is also intellectual poverty – poverty of knowledge. Jesus said, 'Truly I say to you, unless you turn and become like little children you cannot enter the kingdom of God. Whoever humbles himself like this child, he is the greatest in the kingdom of Heaven.'[54] To become like a little child is to realize the incapacity of the mind to understand the truth. The human mind cannot come to the truth but the truth does come to a mind that knows its limitations. Jesus said, 'Father, Lord of heaven and earth! I thank you because you have shown to the unlearned what you have hidden from the wise and the learned. Yes Father, this was how you wanted it to happen.'[55]

Everyone has to become like a little child. Little children are innocent but they are also ignorant, but Jesus was not saying that everyone has to become both ignorant and innocent, but that when one realizes the incapacity of the mind to understand or define the eternal truth, one becomes both innocent and wise. The wise men who came to see the infant Jesus were old, but they were like little children and looked to the sky for wisdom to be manifested. Blessed are those who have realized the limitation of knowledge in trying to understand the truth, for theirs is the kingdom of God, that is, the kingdom of wisdom.

The Scribes and the Pharisees were experts in the scriptures and the law, rich in knowledge but poor in wisdom. Jesus was freed from the burden of knowledge when he discovered the kingdom of God and came to live by wisdom. Wisdom says, 'Come to me all of you who are tired from carrying heavy loads, and I will give you rest. Take my yoke upon you and learn from me that I am meek and humble of heart and you will find rest for your souls. For my yoke is easy and my burden is light.'[56]

Chapter 6

For they will be comforted, they will inherit the earth

Mourning is a state of poverty. We mourn when we lose some-body on whom we are emotionally or economically dependent. A wife mourns when her husband dies and a husband mourns when his wife dies. Parents mourn when their children die and children mourn when their parents die. Jesus said, 'Blessed are those who mourn, they will be comforted. For them it is easy to find the kingdom of God.' When people mourn they realize that much of their happiness is a passing happiness that comes from others and is not the real happiness that comes from God alone. A small story can illustrate the truth that people who lose their earthly source of happiness may realize its passing nature and so find eternal happiness.

Once there was a very beautiful tree. It had lovely branches, which provided a cool shade. The tree yielded sweet fruits and hundreds of people came to admire its lovely branches, take shelter and enjoy its cool shade and sweet fruit. The tree was very impressed by the devotion of its admirers and wanted to attract more. So it began to enlarge its branches, beautify itself and yield more fruits. Hundreds of admirers came, increasing in numbers to thousands, and the tree was very happy.

As days passed the tree began to grow old and its branches began to fall. It became ugly and eventually could no longer yield any fruit. Slowly people stopped coming to the tree and it stood there alone and deserted. One day some villagers were passing by and one of them looked at the old tree and said, 'Look at that tree. How beautiful it once was, how soothing its cool shade used to be, how sweet were its fruits. How many thousands of people used to come to that tree, and now look at it, how ugly it is. We don't even want to look at it.' The tree heard these words and began to weep. It then heard a voice, 'O my tree, O my tree, why are you weeping?' The tree thought that someone had come to see it, so it said, 'When I was young, when I was beautiful, when I gave cool shade and yielded sweet fruit, thousands of people came to me. Now I am old and useless and nobody comes to me; all have deserted me and I feel lonely and unwanted.'

As it said this, the tree looked for whoever had spoken, but there was no one outside. So the tree said in a loud voice, 'Who was it that spoke to me. I do not see anyone!' The voice said, 'O my tree, I am not speaking from outside, but I am speaking from within you. Look within your branches and you will find me.' The tree was surprised; it looked into its branches and there found a bird living in a nest. So the tree asked, 'O my bird, when did you come to me, I have never seen you before.' The bird replied, 'O my tree, I have been living with you from the beginning of your life, but you were so busy with your outside admirers you had no time to feel my presence, to hear my voice.' The tree felt so happy and said, 'My friend, I am very sorry. I thought my admirers would always be with me. Now I realize that they only came to me for as long as I was useful to them. The moment I became useless they left me. You are my real and eternal friend. You did not leave me when everyone else did. You are my faithful and eternal friend.'

Each one of us is the tree and the bird is God who is living in each one of us, whether we want him to or not. He is there whether we recognize him or not. Our real life is living with the realization of that eternal and permanent reality within us. According to Jesus, people who mourn are much closer to finding eternal happiness, that is, the kingdom of God, than people who are laughing now. Blessed are those who mourn for they will discover the kingdom of God living in them. When Jesus said, 'I pity you who are laughing now, for you will mourn and weep,' he was referring to people who find security outside themselves and who have no happiness within them. Their life is in seeking pleasure through the repetition of past memories and experiences. Jesus pitied these people because he saw that, in the end, they would realize that even if they lived for a hundred years, they would not have lived even one second of their lives in reality. Such a life is like the wasted effort of a drunken man who got into a boat tied to the shore and rowed all night until dawn broke and he saw that he was still tied to the shore.

Of course, Jesus was not cursing such people; he was showing them the reality of their situation. He was telling them, 'How I pity you who are laughing now because the day will come when you will realize that your whole life has been a waste; then your laughter will turn into mourning.' He was pointing out that those who mourn now will realize the futility of dependency on external sources of happiness and seek eternal happiness, which is the kingdom of God. Their mourning will turn to laughter.

'Blessed are the meek for they shall inherit the earth' is the same as saying, 'Blessed are the meek for yours is the kingdom of heaven.' Meekness is a poverty of human existence. It is the poverty of power, for the meek are those who are powerless. The so-called powerful people of the world are really powerless, for their power is dependent upon others. A king's power is dependent on his subjects, whom he has to control to remain in power, and a dictator may have to resort to violence to control the people on whom his power depends. If he has a hundred million subjects then his power is dependent on a hundred million subjects and to remain in power he has to control a hundred million people. He lives in constant fear of losing his power or even his life so he feeds the army well hoping that it does not rebel against him. All presidents and prime ministers are dependent upon the people; although they appear to be powerful externally, inside, deep down, they are insecure and powerless.

Jesus spoke to those who are meek and who know they are powerless. It is easy for them to surrender to God and experience his power. Paradoxically, those who are meek and who appear powerless are in fact powerful internally because earthly power is passing and has no eternal value. Those who seek power outside themselves build their houses on sand. The rain and wind come and eventually the houses fall. Those who build their houses on the power of God build their houses on rock. Real power belongs to God and truth is a house built on a rock; externally it may appear meek, weak and vulnerable, but its foundations are strong. On the other hand a house built on sand may appear to be strong and powerful on the outside but in reality it is weak.

The Scribes and the Pharisees were powerful in that they had the power of spiritual knowledge and the scriptures. The priests had the power of the temple. Herod was powerful because of his political power. Jesus did not have the power of the scriptures and the temple, or political power. He was apparently powerless, but his life and message placed the 'powerful' people in a state of crisis. The power of Jesus did not come from the authority of the temple or from political inheritance; it came from wisdom, from God. His power was that which makes everyone free and which gives life. 'Just as the Father has life in himself, he has granted the son to have life in himself.'[57] 'I have come to give life, life in all its fullness.'[58]

When Jesus was going to Jerusalem he sent his disciples

ahead to a Samaritan village to 'prepare everything for him'. But the people would not receive him because he was going to Jerusalem, the centre of the Jews. The Samaritans had nothing in common with the Jews, and maybe they thought that Jesus was going to announce the supremacy of Jerusalem, which would have been a great blow to them. The disciples were very upset about the rebuttal of Jesus by the Samaritans, and James and John said, 'Lord, do you want us to call fire down from heaven to destroy them?'[59] We are familiar with violence committed in the name of God, in the name of religion, in the name of Christ and Christianity, and in the name of the various beliefs within Christianity. Not only were there divisions between the Jews and the Samaritans of two thousand years ago, but these same divisions are still within Christianity. Jesus did not need to resort to violence; rather he turned, rebuked the disciples and went onto another village. Truth does not use violence; it does not need an army. Truth does not need to conquer anything because it has already conquered. Violence is born of fear, fear is born of insecurity and insecurity is born of rigid definitions of the truth.

Whereas a person living in truth has chosen life and the way of insecurity, someone seeking to define truth chooses death, for to define truth is to crucify truth. Truth cannot be imposed as this would involve violence, rather truth invites people to life and every person has the responsibility of accepting or rejecting this invitation for themselves. We know that clouds are weak, that they do not have a permanent foundation and that when their power disappears the sun alone remains. The sun does not fight with the clouds; it does not use violence.

Herod, the Scribes and the Pharisees all used violence. Herod was afraid of the child Jesus, and wanted him out of the way at any cost. He was insecure and fearful so he ordered every male child of Jesus' age in Bethlehem to be killed. Some of the Pharisees, Scribes and priests were also insecure and fearful, so they became violent and killed Jesus. They had defined truth whereas Jesus had no definition of truth, he had nothing to defend, nothing to propagate. He just announced that eternal life is already present in every person. The fact that some people refuse life and freedom and want to remain in their own self-made prisons is illustrated in the parable of the vineyard owner who let his vineyard out to tenants:

> When the time came he sent a servant to the tenants, that they should give him some of the fruit of the vineyard, but the tenants beat him, and sent him away empty handed. He sent another servant, him also they treated shamefully, and sent him away empty handed. And he sent a third, this one they wounded and cast out. Then the owner of the vineyard said, 'What shall I do? I will send my beloved son, it may be that they will respect him.' But when the tenants saw him they said to themselves, 'This is the heir, let us kill him that the inheritance may be ours.' And they cast him out of the vineyard and killed him. What will the owner of the vineyard do to them? He will come and destroy those tenants, and give the vineyard to others. When they heard this they said, 'God forbid.'[60]

God is the owner of the vineyard, he is the absolute. The tenants represent 'relative' truth and are at the service of the absolute. When the relative tries to define its own truth and take the place of the absolute it becomes evil and produces violence. The absolute does not fight, its power is in its 'being', whereas the relative has no power of its own. The meek are those who do not have the power of violence. Their power is rooted in the absolute and ultimately they will inherit the vineyard. Blessed are the meek for theirs is the kingdom of heaven.

Chapter 7

Blessed are those who hunger

Jesus went on to talk of those who hunger and thirst for right-eousness. In Matthew's Gospel he said, 'Blessed are those who hunger and thirst for righteousness, for they will be filled.' In Luke's Gospel Jesus said, 'Blessed are you who are hungry now for you will be filled.'

We feel hunger and thirst and, just as we have to eat each day, in our relationship with God we need to ask him to give us 'our daily bread and drink'. God provides only for today, only for the present, because tomorrow does not exist in God's eyes. We have to ask for truth each moment, as truth cannot be possessed once and for all.

God is more than everything that has been revealed. He is like a mighty and ever-flowing river, whereas that which has been revealed is like a pot of water from the river; a pot of water cut off from the living river is dead – it begins to stagnate. People who are hungry and thirst for living water have to go to the river to drink each day. No one can gather enough living water for his or her whole life. God gives living water only for today.

People who hunger and thirst for God have tasted God, have eaten God, yet hunger for him every day. This is a healthy condition in the spiritual life. In the Kena Upanishad the sage says, 'He who knows him (God), does not know him, but only he who says, "I know him yet I do not know him," knows him.' Such people are always hungry and thirsty for God, and for righteousness. God does not assuage their hunger once and for all rather he gives them their daily food and drink. Such people ask God only for daily food and drink because to be in the kingdom of God is to live in the present, the 'now' of eternity. People who hunger and thirst for righteousness have no psychological tomorrow, only a psychological present. Their hunger and thirst for God is always filled but it is also empty. In one sense they are rich and in another they are poor. Their poverty is their wealth and their wealth is their poverty.

Every religion provides a certain understanding of God and of humanity's relationship with God. Every religion claims to contain the full truth. But people who have defined the truth, who think that God has revealed everything, and that there is nothing left to reveal, are not hungry and thirsty for God's righteousness. Truth is beyond all religions. Truth is beyond all intellectual and theological systems. People who realize that truth is beyond revealed scriptures are blessedly poor; they know what God has given them, but they do not presume to know what God is going to give them. These are people who know and yet do not know; they are hungry and thirsty for righteousness and the kingdom of God belongs to them.

Nicodemus was a Pharisee but unlike other Pharisees he realized that the law was relative and not absolute. He realized that Jesus had something new that could open the door for him and help him in his spiritual crisis, but he was afraid to go to Jesus publicly. So Nicodemus went to Jesus at night and said, 'Rabbi, we know that you are a teacher sent by God. No one could perform the miracles you are doing unless God were with him.' Jesus told him that no one could see the kingdom of God unless he was born again. Nicodemus could not understand what this new birth was, thinking of it as one would a physical birth, and he said, 'How can a grown man be born again? Certainly he cannot enter his mother's womb and be born a second time.'

Jesus was talking of spiritual rebirth by which one transcends the Law to be born out of the womb of religion into a direct experience of God in which the spirit takes possession of a person. This experience gives a new identity to a person and becomes his or her guiding light. Nicodemus could not grasp what Jesus was saying, but he was spiritually open and ready. He was free from the traditional conditioning of a closed mind and heart and was hungry and thirsty for righteousness. So Jesus gave him his teaching, describing for him the life of one who is born of the Spirit. 'Do not be surprised because I tell you that you must be born again. The wind blows wherever it wishes, you hear the sound it makes, but you do not know where it comes from or where it is going. It is like that with everyone who is born of the Spirit.'[61]

The Samaritan woman that Jesus met at Jacob's well also was open spiritually and was hungry and thirsty for righteousness. She entered into a discussion with Jesus and gradually came to realize that Jesus was the Messiah she was waiting for. Jesus gave her a profound teaching:

> But the time is coming and already is here, when by the power of God's spirit, people will worship the Father as he really is, offering him the true worship that he wants. God is spirit and only by the power of his spirit can people worship him as he really is.[62]

The Scribes and the Pharisees were not hungry and thirsty for truth and were satisfied with what had been revealed. They did not expect anything new, indeed they did not want to know anything new, rather they wanted to find fault with Jesus. They tried provoking him into saying something unlawful by which they might catch him out and accuse him:

> Some Pharisees came to Jesus and started to argue with him. They wanted to trap him, so they asked him to perform miracles to show that God approved of him. But Jesus gave a deep groan and said, 'Why do people of this day ask for a miracle? No such proof will be given to these people.'[63]

On another occasion some Pharisees and members of Herod's party were sent to Jesus to trap him with questions:

> Teacher, we know that you tell the truth, without worrying what people think. You pay no attention to men's status but teach them the truth about God's will for man. Tell us; is it against our Law to pay taxes to the Roman Emperor? Should we pay them or not?' Jesus saw through their trick and answered, 'Why are you trying to trap me? Bring me a silver coin and let me see it.' They brought him one and he asked, 'Whose face and name are these?' 'The Emperor's!' they answered. Jesus said, 'Well then, pay the Emperor what belongs to the Emperor and pay to God what belongs to God.' They were amazed at Jesus.[64]

In the same way some Sadducees, who not did believe in the resurrection, came to Jesus and asked him about what would happen to a man in heaven if he died leaving a wife and no children:

> Teacher, Moses wrote for us that if a man's brother dies, having a wife but no children, the man must take the wife and raise up children for his brother. Now there were seven brothers; the first took a wife and died without children. The second and the third took her and likewise all seven left no children and died. Afterwards the woman also died. In the resurrection therefore whose wife will the woman be? For the seven had her as wife.'[65]

The situation described in the story might have been a frivolous invention but Jesus was serious about eternal life and eternal truth, and gave a serious answer:

> The sons of this age marry and are given in marriage, but those who are accounted worthy to attain to that age and to the resurrection from the dead neither marry nor are given in marriage because they cannot die any more, because they are equal to angels and are sons of God, being the sons of the resurrection. But the dead are raised, even Moses showed, in the passage about the bush, where he calls the Lord the God of Abraham, and the God of Isaac and the God of Jacob. Now he is not God of the dead, but of the living, for all live to him.' But there were some of the group of Sadducees who were open and who were ready to learn, who were hungry and thirsty, and they said to Jesus, 'Teacher, you have spoken well,' for they no longer dared to ask him any more questions.[66]

On another occasion a lawyer stood up to put Jesus to the test. He was not really looking for an answer, for the truth, rather he wanted to justify himself. But again Jesus took the question seriously and came out with the truth in such a way as the lawyer was forced to accept it:

> Teacher, what shall I do to inherit eternal life?' He said to him, 'What is written in the Law? How do you read?' And he answered, 'You shall love the Lord your God with all your heart, with all your soul, with all your strength and with all your mind, and your neighbor as yourself.' He said to him, 'You have answered right. Do this and you will live.' But the lawyer, desiring to justify himself, went on to say to Jesus, 'And who is my neighbor?' Then Jesus told him the story of the Good Samaritan, after which he asked the man, 'Which of the three do you think proved neighbor to the man who fell among the robbers?' He said, 'The one who showed mercy,' and Jesus said, 'Go and do likewise.'[67]

The Gospels are full of stories in which people who thought they possessed truth but who did not hunger and thirst for righteousness, wanted to discredit Jesus. In Matthew the Pharisees saw Jesus and his disciples walking through a corn-field on the Sabbath, plucking and eating ears of grain. They said, 'Look, your disciples are doing what is not lawful on the Sabbath.'[68] When Jesus was in the synagogue, there was a man with a withered hand and to accuse him of wrongdoing the Pharisees asked Jesus, 'Is it lawful to heal on the Sabbath?'[69] Jesus healed the man and the Pharisees, convinced that they had the truth, went away and planned his death. They did not want to learn anything new.

Jesus saw that ordinary people were hungry and thirsty for God's will and were closer to the kingdom of God than the Scribes and the Pharisees. He looked at the poor and said, 'Blessed are you who hunger and thirst for righteousness, for you will be filled.' To those who thought they knew God he said, 'How I pity you who are full now, you will discover that you have no life in you. You are dead.' He told those who want-ed to see a sign, 'Some people seek proof and do not have minds that are open to learning... how I pity you who are full now, for you will be hungry.'[70]

Chapter 8

Blessed are the merciful

To be merciful is to be non-judgmental and compassionate and Jesus told his followers that they should not judge other people and in return they would not be judged themselves, 'Condemn not and you will not be condemned. Forgive and you will be forgiven. Give and it will be given to you; good measure, pressed down, shaken together, running over, will be put into your lap, for the measure you give will be the measure you get back.'[71]

To be merciful one has to admit one's poverty in the understanding of truth. A person who has realized that truth cannot be defined has no standard by which to judge others whereas the person who has defined truth will use that definition to judge others. Someone who has realized that truth cannot be defined becomes merciful and non-judgmental. He or she has no image or definition of God, and so has no internal definition with which to judge another person. A person who has realized the truth experiences God as unconditional love, merciful and non-judgmental. A person who defines the truth judges himself or herself by that definition. Jesus said, 'Pay attention to what you hear! The same rules you use to judge others will be used by God to judge you, but with even greater severity.'[72]

Love is merciful, compassionate and non-judgmental. One

has to purify one's perception of reality to see truth. One needs clear eyes, a mind unconditioned by prejudice and a pure heart to take the speck out of a brother's eye,

> You hypocrite, first take the log out of your own eye and then you will see clearly to take the speck out of your brother's eye.[73]

God reveals himself as eternal love and we can see that love that changes is not love. Jesus came to tell us that God loves us with unchanging love and that this everlasting love of God for humanity is nothing but God's presence in every human heart. The story of the bird living in the beautiful tree that grew old and sad until it found a bird nesting in its branches, is about God having built his nest in our hearts, whether we like it or not, whether we know it or not. This everlasting love of God for humanity is non-judgmental. God's love cannot say, 'You are a sinner,' or 'I forgive you,' for love that forgives belongs to time and space, and is not eternal. God cannot say. 'I forgive you,' he can only say. 'I love you with an everlasting love.' This everlasting love of God is seen in the parable that Jesus told of the prodigal son, who squandered his inheritance:

> When he had spent everything a great famine arose in that country and he began to be in need. So he went and worked for one of the citizens of that country who sent him into the fields to feed swine. He would gladly have fed on the pods that the swine ate; but no one gave him anything. When he came to himself he said, 'How many of my father's hired servants have bread enough and to spare, but I perish here with hunger! I will arise and go to my father, and I will say to him, 'Father I have sinned against heaven and before you; I am no longer worthy to be called your son, treat me as one of your hired servants.' And he rose and came to his father. While he was yet at a distance, his father saw him and had compassion, ran, embraced him and kissed him. The son said to him, 'Father I have sinned against

heaven and before you. I am not longer worthy to be called your son.' But the father said to his servants, 'Bring quickly the best robe and put it on him. Put a ring on his hand, shoes on his feet. Bring the fatted calf and kill it, let us eat and make merry. For this my son was dead, and is alive again. He was lost and is found. And they began to make merry.[74]

The prodigal son told his father, 'Father I have sinned against God and against you. I am not worthy to be called your son. Treat me as one of your hired servants.' But the father did not hear anything that his son said. It was as if the father was blind and deaf. The son thought of himself as a sinner returning to the father, but the father did not see a sinner returning; he saw his son. When the son said, 'I have sinned against God,' the father said, 'Bring the best robe and put it on him.' When the son said, 'I have sinned against you,' the father said, 'Put a ring on his finger.' When the son said, 'I am not worthy to be called a son,' the father said, 'Put shoes on his feet.' When the son said, 'Treat me as your hired servant,' the father said, 'Get a prized calf, kill it, and let us celebrate with a feast.'

The father did not once say, 'My son I forgive you.' This is the eternal love with which the father loves his creation. In this love there is no place for forgiveness, because God is too gentle to call someone a 'sinner'. Even when the first parents, Adam and Eve, committed sin, God did not accuse them. When they told him, 'We are naked and ashamed,' he only said, 'Who told you that you are naked? Have you eaten the fruit which I have forbidden you to eat? Only then do you realize that you are naked and feel ashamed.' God could have said, 'I know that you have eaten the fruit which I have forbidden you to eat; you have committed a sin, you are sinners, ask my forgiveness.' God cannot send anyone away from his house.

Human beings, however, can and do choose to leave his garden, but God allows that to happen in the infinite hope that one day they will return.

God is too gentle to condemn anyone as a sinner. He may ask the prophets to tell people that they are sinners, or he may ask the priests to hear the sins of people and forgive them, but God himself cannot call anyone a sinner and cannot say, 'I forgive you.' God can see and hear everything except sin; the one thing that God is deaf and blind to is *sin*.

One needs to be meek, humble and powerless to proclaim the everlasting love of God. Only the Son of God, who is meek, powerless and merciful, can proclaim the everlasting love of God that transcends sin and forgiveness. On the other hand, it needs a person of strength to be a prophet or to be a priest for it takes strength to say, 'You are a sinner', or 'I forgive you.' Christianity has been obsessed with sin and forgiveness, and it is this more than anything that makes people leave the church. Things would have been different if Christianity had been obsessed with the message of God's everlasting love over the years. We have to remember that love is eternal and sin is temporal; sin will come to an end but love has no end.

Blessed are the merciful for they will receive mercy. Blessed are the compassionate for they will receive compassion. The story of the Scribes and the Pharisees bringing to Jesus a woman who had been caught in adultery is a wonderful story of Jesus the merciful and compassionate man. The Scribes and the Pharisees challenged Jesus to condemn the sinner:

> Jesus bent down and wrote with his finger on the ground. And they continued to ask him; he stood up and said to them, 'Let him who is without sin among you be the first to throw a stone at her.' And once more he bent down and wrote with his finger

on the ground. When they heard what he said they went away, one by one, beginning with the eldest, and Jesus was left alone with the woman standing before him. Jesus looked up and said to her, 'Woman where are they? Has no one condemned you?' She said, 'No one Lord.' And Jesus said, 'Neither do I condemn you; go now and do not sin again.'[75]

Chapter **9**

Blessed are the pure in heart, the peacemakers and the persecuted

To see God requires purity of heart and mind. God reveals himself and at the same time he hides himself. To see God one has to be free from past conditioning, for God is always new and the mind that projects its conditioning onto God only sees what God was and not what God is.

Jesus likened the eyes to a lamp for the body. When the eyes are sound the whole body is full of light, when the eyes are no good the whole body is in darkness. Make certain then that the light in you is not darkness. 'If your whole body is full of light, with no part of it in darkness, it will be bright all over, as when a lamp shines on you with its brightness.'[76]

Jesus was speaking of the inner eye rather than the physical eye, the eye of the heart, and the eye of the mind. A conditioned mind and heart cannot experience God who is unconditional love. The human mind and heart can be conditioned culturally, nationally, ethnically, religiously, linguistically, because of one's gender, and in many other ways. If one identifies with one's particular religious or ethnic group, with one particular color of skin or sex, one cannot see God. One has to become a universal man or woman, the Son of God or the Daughter of God, in whom God can see the whole of humanity, the whole of creation. Unless one's individual consciousness grows into the universal consciousness one cannot see God in his or her completeness, one can only see the God of one's own projections.

God has two aspects; the historical and immanent, and the eternal and transcendent. When Moses encountered God he asked God his name. God answered, 'I am who I am,' which is to say, 'I do not have any name; there is no other reality outside me by which I describe myself. I am the only God, there is no other God besides me.' The reply reveals the transcendent and eternal aspect of God. But it is impossible to communicate with this transcendent aspect of God and no relationship is possible. God then said to Moses, 'Say to the Israelites that the Lord, the God of your fathers, the God of Abraham, the God of Isaac, and the God of Jacob, has sent me to you. This is my name forever.'[77] The God who is named is the immanent or manifested God, the God who communicates with his people, the God who reveals, the God of history who manifests in time. But God is more than that which he or she has revealed. God remains transcendent.

The transcendent God is like an ever-flowing river and the immanent God, the God we have named, the God of memory, is like a pot of water taken from the river. The people following Moses in the desert were only able to recognize the God of their memory, the God they could communicate with and with whom they could have a relationship. But God always transcends memory with his eternal aspect, the 'I am', which goes beyond space and time. Communication with the transcendent aspect is possible only through communion, the encounter of emptiness with emptiness, nakedness with nakedness. It is a profound and intimate relationship. It is a relationship between the essential natures of God and a human being. It may be that words might come out of communion but such words have a liberating quality.

God created humanity in his or her own image and likeness. This means there is a transcendent aspect, a transcendent mystery in every person. There is an 'I am' which is without a name, without form, without clothes, naked and empty. This is the natural and essential aspect of every human being that cannot be put under the control of the mind. There is also an acquired and artificial aspect of each person which has a particular name, a particular color, a particular sex, a particular nationality, a particular language, a particular religion, a particular age and particular psychological disposition, all of which makes a person unique. Everything that separates us from others is artificial and does not belong to the transcendent aspect of our being. They are what we *have* and not what we *are*. All our relationships with God, and with one another, are based on these immanent aspects, on names and forms, which give us a sense of belonging, but at the same time are the cause of separation and conflict. Human beings are not created to settle into names and forms. They are created to be on the path of discovering their transcendent aspect, which alone gives final fulfillment.

Just as we can say who God *was* but never who God *is* we can never say who a person *is*, the *now* of a person, the *present* of a person. We can only say who a person *was*, the *past* of a person. The *now* of a person always remains a mystery. We know what God revealed, what God did in the past, but the *present* of God is always a mystery, always transcendent. Only in our transcendent mystery, the 'I am', can we enter into communion with the transcendent mystery of God, '*I am*'.

Jesus entered the Jewish experience of God. He entered the

Jewish memory of God, the God of Abraham, the God of Isaac and the God of Jacob. But the God of Jesus is not only the God of Abraham but is also the God of eternity, for he transcends Abraham. 'Before Abraham was, I am.' The God of Jesus was the God of the past, the God of memory, but is also the God of today. In Jesus the God of history and the God of eternity are one. The transcendent God and the immanent God are one. The God of memory separates us from others, but the God of eternity unites us with the whole of humanity. To experience the God of today one needs purity of mind and heart and one has to be free from the God of memory, the immanent God, the God of Abraham, Isaac and Jacob to encounter the God who is before Abraham.

Jesus then said, 'Blessed are the peacemakers for they will be called the children of God.'[78] To be a peacemaker one has to be completely poor, open and impartial. Imagine an inter-religious conference at which there are Christians, Muslims, Buddhists, Jains, Hindus and representatives of other religious traditions. The people at the conference want to bring unity and peace among themselves but it is not clear that any one of them could be the person to do this. If a Christian were to be appointed to the role of peacemaker he may be partial to the Christians or if a Hindu were appointed he might show preference to the Hindus. Similarly a Muslim might show preference to the Muslims and a Buddhist might show preference to the Buddhists. Only a man or woman who did not belong to any of these groups could be the peacemaker they are looking for.

Peacemakers are called children of God, and as children of God they have a love for all children of God. To be a peacemaker one has to be completely free from any conditioning. Truth cannot be defined and every system that tries to define truth kills the truth. Nobody can take a pot of water from the ever-flowing river of truth and say, 'this is the river'. Only the truth, the river itself, can bring peace amongst the pots of water showing up their limitations and by inviting them to flow again with the living stream. All our ideas about God, our religions, are like nests in which we receive security, protection and nourishment until our wings are grown and we can take flight into the eternal. If our descriptions of God become definitions and we stop people flying the nest into the eternal, these definitions become cages that stop humanity growing to its full potential. 'Peace I leave with you, my peace I give to you, not as the world gives do I give to you. Let not your hearts be troubled, neither let them be afraid.'[79] 'I have said this to you that in me you may have peace. In the world you have tribulation, be of good cheer. I have overcome the world.'[80] Blessed are the peacemakers for they shall be called the children of God.

Jesus then said, 'Blessed are those who are persecuted for righteousness sake, for theirs is the kingdom of heaven.'[81] This insight can be explained with the story of why the bat flies at night.

> Once upon a time animals and birds were living together as one family. One day a conflict arose between them and they were divided into two groups, birds and animals. They fixed a time when each one had to choose to join either the birds or the animals. However a bat refused to take sides saying, 'We are one family and we should remain one family, we should not separate.' When the time for choosing came the bat went to the side of the birds but they chased him away. Then he went to the side of the animals but they chased him away. Both the birds and the animals persecuted the bat and so it is that it remains in hiding during the day and comes out only at night.

Blessed are those who are persecuted for righteousness sake for theirs is the kingdom of God. To belong to the kingdom means to belong to the whole of humanity. To belong to a group might make one rich and secure but it also makes one feel insecure and fearful and creates conflicts between groups. Not belonging to any group leaves one feeling alone, but in that aloneness one realizes the 'all-oneness' (aloneness). Blessed are those who are 'all-one' (alone) for theirs is the kingdom of heaven.

Many dehumanizing persecutions have been carried out in the name of religion, color, race and sex throughout human history. One religion persecuting other religious minorities, one race persecuting another race, one ethnic group persecuting another ethnic group, one sex trying to persecute the other sex, one Christian denomination persecuting its own members as heretics. All this has been done in the name of religion. Persecution arises when people identify themselves with the accidental aspects of human nature and make an absolute out of those aspects. One sees others as enemies and tries to destroy them, and the majority try to persecute the minority as if they are a threat to them. This happened in the early history of Christianity when Christians were persecuted. Later, when Christianity became the majority religion, it became oppressive, burning people at the stake, condemning them to hell. This tendency is not found in all religions, but throughout our modern world persecutions and killings take place in the name of God, in the name of an ethnic group, in the name of a tribe, or in the name of a religion, nationality or culture.

Truth is unconditional love and transcends all these conditionings. People who are filled with unconditional love do not identify themselves with the accidental aspects of human nature. They are alone and do not have the security of one group or one religion; they are blessed for although 'persecuted for righteousness sake', theirs is the kingdom of heaven. Jesus did not die for any particular religion, race, language, nationality or culture; he died for all humanity. Jesus broke down the walls of division and created a new humanity. Anybody who is in Christ is in a new creation, in which the whole of humanity and the whole of creation is united, just as a leaf feels its connection to the tree. This is the righteousness to which God invites everybody.

Before Jesus could announce the Good News of the kingdom of God he had to find it within his own life. The kingdom experience breaks down the walls of division between God and creation, between God and humanity and between human beings, and brings peace and harmony. This is the original state of humanity and will be the ultimate state of all human beings. But the human ego builds walls between God and creation, between God and humanity and between human beings. The ego finds security in these divisions, but in so doing drives people away from the kingdom of God. The invitation of Jesus to return to their original home may not be appealing, and may, indeed, appear as a threat to people who are happy in their artificial security. But those who have no security in any artificial house built by the human ego find it easier to respond to the invitation of Jesus.

The essential teaching of the Beatitudes is Jesus sharing his own experience rather than any intellectual teaching. He gave us his own flesh and blood to consume. Jesus was blessed because he was materially and intellectually poor in that he saw the limitation of the human mind. Thus he became like a little child. He was spiritually poor in that he had no desire of his own, no identity of his own. He was humble, meek and powerless. He had a pure heart and mind. He was a peacemaker for he built bridges between humanity and God. He stood for the human potential to transcend religions and discover oneness with God.

The Beatitudes are the personal experience of Jesus, the experience of the kingdom of God, which presents each person with a clear and choice-less choice in which no time is spent considering options, as in the story of the man who found he was sitting on a gold mine:

> Once upon a time a group of friends went in search of a gold mine. They searched for years but never succeeded in finding any gold. One day they were in a thick forest when one of them became sick and could walk no further, so the friends were forced to leave him behind and continued their search for gold. The sick man was very sad and was sitting under a tree thinking about his misfortune, when suddenly he saw a hole in which something appeared to be shining like gold. He immediately started digging in the hole and, taking away the mud, found that he was sitting on a gold mine.

Humanity is walking on the gold mine of the kingdom of God but does not know it. Jesus came to reveal the eternal truth that the kingdom of God is everywhere, stop your searching and find that you are already in it. Blessed are you who have failed to find the kingdom because it is easy for you to realize that you are already in it.

Part **3**

A new Christianity

Is it so Lord?
Is it so Lord that you have kept
the image of your beauty
in the fading beauty of the world
so that it may direct us to you?
Is it so Lord that you have kept
The flash of your unending bliss
in the fleeting pleasures of the world
so that they may lead us to you?
Is it so Lord that you have kept
the image of your unending union with us
in the ending union of a man and woman
so that it may point us to you?
Is it so Lord that you have kept
the image of your infinity in us
in our unending desire to live
so that it may lead us to you, the true life?
Is it so Lord that you have kept
the image of your eternal life in us
in our desire to be young always
so that it may lead us to you, the eternally young?

Chapter **10**

The cage becomes a nest

Jesus came to establish a new heaven and a new earth. He came to break down walls of division and to create a new humanity, a humanity that would be in harmony with God. But two thousand years later the world is just as divided and Christ himself has become a source of division between Christianity and other religions, as well as between Christians themselves. Tremendous violence has been, and continues to be, done in the name of Christ and Christianity. In our times efforts have been made to bring about unity between Christians in the name of ecumenism, and to bring about unity between religions in the name of inter-religious dialogue. However, these efforts have not led to unity but rather.to a call to accept Christian and religious pluralism and for people to learn to co-exist. It seems that there is no way out.

How can it be that Jesus who came to break down the walls of division is a source of division? The purpose of any religion is to liberate people, give them happiness and make their spiritual life light. When a religion does not do this it becomes a monstrous evil and a force that oppresses people, generation after generation, century after century. To help answer this question we can look at the difference between two types of revelation. The first is objective revelation in which God reveals what humanity should do and should not do. This was the revelation that God gave to the people of Israel through Moses. But this is only a preparation for a second, more profound revelation in which God reveals *who we are*. By this second revelation, the first, which previously had been thought of as absolute, becomes relative. The prophet Jeremiah pointed to this new covenant God would make with the 'people of Israel and the people of Judah':

> It will not be like the old covenant that I made with their ancestors when I took them by the hand and led them out of Egypt. Although I was like a husband to them they did not keep that covenant. The new covenant that I will make with the people of Israel will be this. I will put my law within them, and write it on their hearts.[82]

Jesus inaugurated the new covenant, which God had promised through the prophets, at his baptism. The heavens opened and the Spirit of God came upon Jesus and he discovered who he *was*. 'You are my beloved Son' was a revelation that became a light by which Jesus had to live his life. 'God gave the Law through Moses but grace and truth came through Jesus Christ.'[83]

This new revelation is a gift given by God to the whole of humanity from all eternity. It is truth because it unites humanity with God whereas the law separates humanity from God and creates duality. Truth unites humanity with God and establishes non-duality. Truth and the law, duality and non-duality belong to different orders and cannot be mixed.

> No one uses a piece of new cloth to patch up an old coat, because the new patch will shrink and tear off some of the old cloth, making an even bigger hole. Nor does anyone pour new wine into used wineskins because the wine will burst the skins and both the wine and the skins will be ruined. Instead new wine must be poured into fresh wineskins.[84]

This new covenant was not really new for it is in fact the eternal covenant, the original covenant that God made when he created humanity. In this sense the new covenant is eternal and original, and represents a consciousness that was with mankind at the time of creation, but became lost until rediscovered by Jesus. In this new covenant there is no objective code written on tablets of stone, but a code written by the spirit of God in the heart of every woman and man. The law written on tablets of stone makes the human heart hard as stone, cruel and without mercy, flexibility and compassion. The law written on stone is like a statue carved in stone, always the same, never changing. It has ears and cannot hear, it has legs but cannot walk, it has hands but cannot help. It is a burden, as it has to be carried by people.

Human life requires constant changes as circumstances change and in this context the written law is helpless, and can be said to kill life. But the law written by God in the human heart is flexible and compassionate and ready to change according to the 'signs of the times'. With this law God does not write anything down for one can write on stone only because it has no life, one cannot write on a living heart. It is no more possible to write on the living heart than it is to write on water.

The conflict between Jesus and the religious authorities of his time was the conflict between the heart of stone and the heart of flesh, between the law that takes away life and the truth that gives life, between the law which is a burden to be carried and the life that frees men and women from all burdens. The objective law is like a nest, a refuge in which one can grow and be given security until one discovers one's original state, the real 'I', which is the image and likeness of God in every human being, a gift God gives to each one of us from all eternity. This is what God has created and what God has created he has already saved. This is the hidden treasure, the precious pearl, buried in the heart of every man and woman.

The ego is not the creation of God; it is the creation of the human mind through ignorance, and it is bondage from which the human mind has to liberate itself so that it can discover the truth and the grace of God. The law comes into existence with the ego and since this has no ultimate existence the law based on the ego has no ultimate value. The problem comes when the written law, which is relative, becomes absolute and in so doing transforms the nest into a cage, a prison that blocks the human potential to discover the hidden treasure. Every human being has the potential to fly from the nest into the freedom of infinite space.

The religious authorities at the time of Jesus had made the religious law absolute and transformed the nest into a cage. Religious law is not itself bad, indeed it is necessary, but it becomes evil when it becomes absolute. Humanity is not condemned to live by an external code for all eternity, but is invited to use the law as a ladder to climb towards infinite freedom. Ladders are meant for climbing up and not for sitting upon. When people sit down on a ladder they neither enter infinite freedom themselves nor do they allow others to climb and enter life. They become an obstacle for the spiritual growth of people.

When religion based on the written law is a nest the mother bird watches joyfully as her little ones fly into the freedom of infinite space. But when it is a cage it becomes a prison with guards who control the doors, who provide daily sustenance but see that the birds do not leave. It punishes those birds that question the absolute nature of the cage and try to leave. The law creates a duality between the 'righteous' and the 'unrighteous', those who are inside the cage and those who are outside. Inside the cage there is security, protection, nourishment but there is no life. Outside the bird that has flown into the infinite has no security, is vulnerable, but he or she has life full of infinite possibilities. Whereas a cage has doors and guards, a nest has no doors and has a mother and a teacher within. Take away the gates and the cage becomes a nest, the guard becomes a mother and a teacher. Religion can be seen as a mother and its greatness is not in the number of children conceived in her maternal womb but rather the number of children she has given birth to into the freedom of infinite space. A mother who wants only to conceive but who does not want to give birth transforms her womb into a tomb, killing her children without giving them the chance of seeing the light of the sun.

Jesus discovered that human beings have the potential to be born again out of the womb of their religion and fly into the freedom of infinite space. He forced himself out of the womb of his religion based on the law and became the first-born of his religion. Jesus was the fulfillment of his religion and he gave the gift of motherhood to Judaism, which until then had been a pregnant woman. He broke open the doors of the cage and transformed it into a nest so that people were again at liberty to fly. Jesus 'relativized' the religion based on the law and the temple and opened the way to religion of internal freedom and infinite life.

> But the hour is coming, and now is, when the true worshippers will worship the Father in spirit and truth, for such the Father seeks to worship him. God is spirit and those who worship him must worship in spirit and truth.[85]

Where there is freedom there is life and where there is no freedom there is no life. From his own experience Jesus saw clearly that humanity was imprisoned in the cage of religion, in the name of God and the name of the law. He was angry with the religious authorities of his time who had the keys to the kingdom of God but who oppressed the people by not entering the kingdom themselves and by not allowing others to come and go. The greatest sin of the law-keepers at any point in human history has been to 'absolutise' the law. Jesus, the way, the truth and the life, is always there to reprove those who make the law absolute. Jesus is always there to liberate people imprisoned in the cage of religion, perhaps even being killed by the guardians of the cage. It is a tragedy that the message of Jesus, which transformed the cage into a nest, has itself been transformed into a cage by the human mind, and that Jesus himself has been used by the law-keepers to imprison people in the cage of Christianity.

Religious law that has been 'absolutized' divides people into two, the righteous and the unrighteous, the just and the sinners. The law cannot bridge this gap, but the message of Jesus is that the righteousness of the kingdom transcends this duality. The righteousness of the kingdom does not come from a strict adherence to the law; it comes as a free gift from God. 'Unless your righteousness surpasses that of the Scribes and the Pharisees you cannot enter into the kingdom of Heaven.'[86] When Jesus saw the poor, the innocent, the oppressed, the rejected, the so-called sinners and the outcast, he had compassion for them. Jesus saw these oppressed people and said:

> Come to me all you who labor and are burdened of heart, I will give you rest. Take my yoke upon you and learn from me, for I am meek and humble of heart and you will find rest for your souls, for my yoke is easy and my burden is light.[87]

His compassion turned to anger with the Scribes and the Pharisees and when he saw the teachers of the law and said, 'How terrible also for you teachers of the law! You put loads on people's backs, which are hard to carry, but you yourselves will not stretch out a finger to help them carry loads.'[88] And he said, 'How terrible for you teachers of the law! You have the keys of the kingdom of Heaven, neither do you enter nor do you allow others to enter.'[89]

Jesus identified his mission with the words of the prophet Isaiah, proclaiming that he has come to announce the Good News to the poor, to free people imprisoned in the name of God, religion and the law, to open the eyes of those who are spiritually blind and to set free those who are oppressed and to announce the year of Jubilee in which all things return to their original state.[90] Jesus came to take away all burdens and to give rest to the human heart.

Chapter **11**

Jesus walks on the water

The miracle of Jesus walking on the water is a prophetic sign for the start of the third millennium. The miracle was not a demonstration of the power of Jesus, the least and last thing he would have thought of doing, rather it has eternal value and an eternal message.

Jesus guided his disciples on the road and the road can be taken to be a symbol of the practical moral code. The road takes one to the sea, to the infinite and the unknown. One cannot make a road on the sea and one has to travel in a boat, which can be taken to symbolise a belief structure to take believers to the other shore. There are many boats in the sea, including many labelled 'Christianity'. Jesus often travelled with his disciples in a boat but at one point he asked his disciples to go ahead in the boat by themselves and he did not go with them. As the boat, with the wind against it, was being tossed about by the waves, Jesus came to his disciples walking on the water.[91]

Perhaps Jesus was revealing a new way of life by his action and was inviting his disciples to follow him. Maybe he was smiling at his disciples, telling them, 'Come to me all you who labour and are struggling. I will give you rest. Look at me and learn from me how light I am. I am empty and ego-less. I can

walk on the water. I do not need any boat. I do not need to
labor and struggle. In me you can find rest for your souls because
my way is not the way of the boat. My way is a way without a
way. In me the way and the destiny are one. My way is my destiny. For this reason my way is very easy. You can be free each
moment of your life, my burden is light.'

The way of Jesus is not *a way* among many other ways to
God. It is not *the only way* that denies other ways to God. It is
not *the perfect way* among imperfect ways. The way of Jesus is
that which transcends all ways, all roads and all boats. To transcend all ways, all religions, is to transcend the ego since ways
belong to the realm of the ego. To walk on the water one must
be light, humble and ego-less because the ego cannot walk on
the water. The ego is like a stone; it is heavy however small it
is. It needs to live by the moral code of a road, and it always
needs a boat of belief in which to travel into the unknown. The
ego that tries to walk on the water will be drowned and the ego
that tries to fly will fall to the ground and break its hands and
legs.

There is only one way to God, and that is to renounce one's
ego. The ultimate purpose of any religion is to help her adher-
ents to leave the ego, but every religion creates her own ego and
every religion has her own boat in the sea of the infinite. Today
there are many boats promising to take people to the other
shore, but every boat separates us from direct contact with the
infinite sea. At the level of the boats there is no solution, there
is no hope for unity of Christians and of religions. Each one will
say, 'My boat is true; my boat will take me to God. I respect
other boats but my boat is good enough for me.'

Our real self, the real 'I', created in the image and likeness
of God, is as light as a feather. This 'I' can walk on the water of

the infinite ocean and can fly into the freedom of the infinite sky. It does not need a road, or a boat, as it is one with its destiny. The way of life of the real 'I' is a life of unfolding, just as the way of the ego is the life of becoming. Just as the fish in the water make their journey without leaving any lasting trace, or the birds fly from morning to evening without leaving any trace in the sky, so also the followers of eternal life live their lives without leaving any lasting trace. In the waters and space of eternal life no one follows traces left by others, and no one leaves traces for others to follow. Each person enters the original space and the original waters; everyone lives an original life. No person will be a master of others and no person will be a disciple of another. Each person will be his or her own master and his or her own disciple.

When the master leaves the boat it means he or she is renouncing his authority and power as a master. Walking on the water is the most humble action a person can make. What can be more humble than for a person to disappear without leaving any traces for others to follow? To leave traces means relegating followers to second-hand human beings and likewise to enter the traces left by another is to become a second-hand human being. A compassionate man or woman can leave traces for others as a pointer, just as those the birds leave on the ground before they fly into the freedom of infinite space. In this sense in eternal life there is no master and no disciple, just as God promised the prophet Jeremiah, 'None of them will have to teach his fellow countryman to know the Lord because all will know me from the least to the greatest.'

The master dies to give life to his disciples. The disciple and the master become friends. Jesus told his disciples, 'No longer do I call you servants for the servant does not know what the master is doing. But I have called you friends for all that I have heard from my Father I have made known to you.'[92] And he said, 'I do not want to call you servants or disciples but I want to call you my friends.' Referring to the hypocrisy of the Scribes and Pharisees, Jesus told his disciples:

> You are not to be called 'Rabbi' for you have one teacher and you are all brethren. And call no man your father on earth, for you have one Father who is in heaven. Nor are you to be called 'master' for you have one master, the Christ. He who is greatest among you shall be your servant. Whoever exalts himself will be humbled and whoever humbles himself will be exalted.[93]

In not going with the disciples in the boat Jesus was renouncing his title of 'master'. Previously he had taken such titles to be a help to the disciples, to bring them face to face with reality, but his intention was then to withdraw from the scene; he was their servant. Walking on the water was Jesus' most humble action, for the most humble thing that any person can do is to not become a model for others and so take away their life. Jesus came to give his life for others, to give life to others, not to take away life. 'Just as the Father has life in himself, so also he has granted the Son to have life in himself.'[94] 'I have come so that you may have life, life in all its fullness.'[95] By walking on the water Jesus was saying to every one of his disciples, and all humanity, 'As long as you are in the boat you will have to struggle and you will never have rest. Only in me can you find rest. Leave the boat and enter the sea of God so that you also may be where I am. If you trust the sea of God, the sea will take care of you. Don't be afraid, you can do that.'

In responding to the call of Jesus Peter did not think he was betraying his companions, and indeed there is no betrayal in the matter of spiritual growth. Peter discovered higher possibilities in his relationship with the master and responded by leaving the boat, his companions and his leadership. He was able to walk on the water, but the experience of freedom was too much for him. His previous self, the ego, returned and he began to drown. Peter was weak psychologically for he was quick to respond but then would retreat. It was as if he was saying to Jesus, 'Though they fall away because of you I will never fall away.' Jesus was later to say to Peter, 'Truly I say to you this very night, before the cock crows, you will deny me three times.' Peter replied, 'Even if I must die with you, I will not deny you.'[96] In the event Peter denied Jesus three times, but he had an open mind and an open heart; he was not rigid, and was quick to perceive the truth. When Jesus asked his disciples, 'Who do you say that I am?' it was Peter who replied, 'You are the Christ, the Son of the living God.' Jesus rewarded Peter for his perception:

> Blessed are you, Simon Bar-Jonah! For flesh and blood has not revealed this to you, but my Father who is in heaven. And I tell you, you are Peter, and on this rock I will build my church, and the power of death shall not prevail against it. I will give you the keys of the kingdom of heaven and whatever you bind on earth shall be bound in heaven and whatever you loose on earth shall be loosed in heaven.[97]

The keys of the kingdom that Jesus gave Peter were not keys that open the gates of the kingdom of heaven (for heaven is everywhere and cannot have gates), but they were keys to open the door of the cage and liberate those imprisoned inside. What keys can be more powerful than those that 'relativize' religion. The keys are wisdom. Jesus gave Peter the wisdom of the kingdom that frees people from the burden of knowledge, the burden of the law and religions. These keys, which were already promised in the scriptures as the new covenant, can only be used to liberate people, not to enslave. Knowledge of the law builds roads and boats of belief structures but wisdom frees people from both the roads and the boats and unites them to God.

Jesus and Peter have a profound truth to reveal for our time, as millions of Christians are leaving the stifling institutional churches and are looking for the inner freedom elsewhere. It is agonizing to see millions of Christians as orphans, knocking on the door of other religions for love and spiritual solace while their mother remains hard-hearted, imprisoning herself within her self-made prison. Jesus revealed the ultimate destiny which humanity has to take. He was as a bird flying in the freedom of the infinite sky, but out of compassion for humanity he came down to earth and left his footprints as a marker to show people that someone has actually flown into the sky. People then built great monuments on the footprints, and completely forgot the destiny Jesus offered to all men and women. Jesus was like a great swimmer who out of compassion for humanity left his clothes on the shore to show that he had entered the infinite ocean of God. But people then built monuments of the clothes and forgot the destiny he took and which he offered to humanity.

As the representative of the disciples, Peter attempted to leave the boat and to become the friend of Jesus, if only for a few minutes. Prophetically he showed the next step the disciples of Jesus had to take. But this step, this path, which is not a path, is narrow and very short.

> Enter by the narrow gate, for the gate is wide and the way is easy that leads to destruction, and those who enter it are many. For the gate is narrow and the way is hard that leads to life, and those who find it are few.[98]

The way to life is narrow, not in the sense of space, but in the sense that this step cannot be taken collectively. Each man and woman has to take this step 'alone'. Each one has to take up his or her cross and follow Jesus. Each one has to leave his or her ego and discover his or her real 'I'. One can travel with one's father or mother, husband or wife, or with one's children on the road or in the boat. This is the wider path, the well-established road, which many people take and along which it is easy to walk for one does not have to make the road as one goes. However, such a journey does not lead to eternal life, for to step into infinite life and freedom one has to leave father, mother, wife, husband and children, at least in an internal sense. To walk with a group is easy, but to walk alone is difficult. To walk on a path made by someone else is to live a second-hand human existence and while this might be acceptable on a physical level, it can be destructive in the spiritual life.

This way is not only narrow, but is also short in the sense that one can only take one step at a time. One only sees *now*, living moment by moment. It is a paradox that the way to infinite life and infinite freedom is narrow and short. It can only be trod by one person at a time and also moment-by-moment. But when one sees clearly that the roads and the boats still belong to the realm of the ego then taking the narrow and short path of the real self becomes a choice-less choice.

Jesus stands on the water and invites everyone who labors and who is burdened of heart to come to him, 'Come to me, I will give you rest. I am the way, the truth and the life. My way is without a boat. Leaving all the boats is my way, and this is the only way to infinite truth and infinite life. My way is easy because the way itself is the destiny, the way itself is the truth, and the way itself is the life. You can find rest for your souls. My burden is light because I do not carry the burden of the written law. My only burden is my infinite freedom, which is not a quantity, but a quality and 'quality' has no weight.'

This is the only hope for humanity, the only hope for unity amongst Christians and for unity of all religions. If the Christian churches were to accept that they are just boats and that Jesus, the truth, is beyond the boats on the water, and if they were to take the place of John the Baptist and say to their followers, pointing to Jesus on the water, 'Behold the lamb of God who takes away the sin of the world,'[99] that would be the end of ecumenism and the beginning of unity. If all religions proclaimed openly that they are just boats and that the truth is beyond them on the water of the infinite ocean, and if they affirmed publicly that human beings are greater than religion, and that they can leave the boats and walk on the water, proclaiming, 'I am the way, the truth and the life,' that would then be the end of inter-religious dialog and the beginning of unity. Such an affirmation would be the beginning of a new earth and a new heaven. Then the prophecy of Jeremiah, which was fulfilled in the time of Jesus, would become a reality in everyone's life.

Chapter 12

Who do you say that I am?

Jesus asked his disciples, 'Who do you say that I am?'[100] He still poses this question to each one of his disciples, and our answer will reveal our destiny, our liberation or our bondage. Every disciple of Jesus has to respond to this question personally.

The human mind always wants to identify with definitions and put truth under its control; it always wants to name the 'other'. This 'other' can be God or a human being or a created thing. Only when it names the other can the mind communicate with the other. For instance, when we meet someone for the first time we ask, 'Who are you, what is your name?' We seek the other's identity because without it the other remains unknown.

When Moses encountered God and asked God his name. First God answered, 'I am who I am,' which is to say, 'I do not have a name. There is no reality outside me by which I describe myself. I am the only God, there is no other God besides me.' In every man and woman there is an 'I am', without name and form, without clothes, empty and naked. This is the natural and essential element of every human being on top of which lie the 'acquired' aspects of name, race, color, sex, personality and psychological disposition.

Each person Jesus encountered would have formed positive

or negative images of him for communication, and relationship would not have been possible without such images. The one common thing was, and this is true today, that the image people formed of Jesus would have been formed through the instrument of their memory. People knew John the Baptist, they had read about or had heard about Elijah, they knew about Jeremiah and the other prophets. They were also expecting a Messiah who would liberate them from the oppression of Roman occupation. The Messiah was their hope.

The past in the form of the prophets, and the future in the form of the Messiah, were already in the memory of the people Jesus met, and this was how they were able to identify him. People projected the past and their hopes for the future onto Jesus. 'Some say you are John the Baptist, others instead say you are the prophet Elijah, and others say that you are one of the old prophets returned.' These were the projections of people other than the disciples, and when Jesus asked his disciples who they thought he was. Peter, representing them, said, 'You are the Christ,'[101] or, 'You are the Christ, the son of the living God.'[102]

Whereas many people projected the past onto Jesus, the disciples projected the future onto him. To see the promised one in Jesus is certainly the action of the grace of God, but this promise was not new and was already predicted in the scriptures. At one stage this projection reflected their image of and their need for a glorious Messiah, a political king who would liberate them from the Romans, who would become a king like David on whose left side and right side would sit his disciples. Jesus accepted Peter's response and praised him,[103] he was really the hope of Israel, but he corrected Peter by saying, 'The Son of Man must suffer much and be rejected by the elders, the chief priests, and the teachers of the law. He will be put to death, but three days later he will be raised to life.'[104] Peter could not accept this and began to rebuke Jesus, saying, 'God forbid Lord! This shall never happen to you.' Jesus then had to say to him, 'Get behind me Satan! You are a hindrance to me, for you are not on the side of God but of men.'[105]

A disciple who projects his ambitions onto the master becomes an obstacle to the master. It is important that disciples should not project their aspirations onto a master, but should leave him or her to be as God wants them to be. The human mind has the tendency to project the past or its hopes for the future onto the present, but we should not project our aspirations and our ambitions onto others or use them as instruments to achieve our personal ambitions. Every human projection onto God becomes a burden to God, and every projection of a disciple onto the master becomes a burden to the master. Projections create clouds between God and humanity, between disciples and a master. People may think that by giving superlative titles to their master they are doing a great service to him or her, but in fact they are doing a disservice. By projecting titles onto a master they create an ideal that is impossible for common people to reach. It also gives tremendous power to those who represent the master, and in this way the master becomes a heavy burden, often an impossible burden, that keeps people in eternal submission and oppression.

A true master comes to free people from all burdens including the burden of the master himself. A true master is meek and humble, refusing any title that creates distance between him or her and the disciples. When people retract their projections of the past and the future, their fears and hopes, then God becomes free, the master becomes free and the disciples also become free. In this freedom human beings discover the transcendent mystery of the other, in which there is no place for a name or for an identity to be given. There is only profound communion, without words, without names and without form. All walls between one human being and another and between God and humanity are broken down. Words may flow from this communion, forms may come and names may be given, but these names give rise to new names, so Abram became Abraham, Jacob became Israel, and Simon became Peter. Words flowing from communion do not divide people but unite them.

Jesus asked God, 'Who am I?' God replied, 'You are my beloved Son.' To give an identity to the Son also means giving an identity to the Father. But in this case such a name does not create a duality, a distance, rather it creates non-duality, they are no longer two but one. This is expressed in the words of Jesus, 'I and the Father are one.'[106] God also asked Jesus, 'Who are you?' and Jesus replied, 'I am your beloved Son.' This response did not come from Jesus' memory, it was an original response Jesus discovered in his direct experience of God when the Spirit came upon him. In the Jewish tradition no one had given this response in the way Jesus did and meant. It was a response that did not create walls but broke down walls and created communion between the Father and the Son.

Jesus asks every person, 'Who am I?' which implies the question, 'Who are you?' In answering this question we either might have the answer in our memory or we might stop our memory. Everything depends upon the answer we give. Our response will be our liberation or our bondage. Do we have the answer already in our memory or if not what answer can we give? Our response will either break down the walls of division or build walls between us.

When Peter said, 'You are the Christ,' this answer came from his memory, for, although there was much debate about the manner of his coming and the nature of his mission, people were expecting a Messiah. To recognize the promised one in Jesus and to affirm it publicly was indeed extraordinary, but the real identity of Jesus transcends all expectations and projections and Jesus was much more than the Messiah. As the manifested or functional aspect of the Son of God, the Messiah has no permanent value for it belongs to the world of time and space. The deepest self of all human beings transcends time and space, and although we are not called to be the Messiah, all human beings are called to be the sons and daughters of God. Peter's answer should not be taken as the only, final and ultimate response to the question that Jesus posed. Peter's response took humanity to a deeper relationship with Christ and God, but at the same time it created an unbridgeable gulf between Christ and Christians. It made communication between Christ and Christians possible but it closed the door to communion.

Peter's identification of Jesus as the Christ can be interpreted in two ways. If it means that every human being can aspire to this identity in his or her spiritual journey, then it is liberating and can be a rock on which each person can build his or her house. If it means the elevation of Jesus to a higher level, condemning humanity to be second grade human beings for all eternity, then it is oppressive and cannot be a rock on which each one of us can build his or her house.

By identifying Jesus as the Christ of God, and later the Son of God, Christians have taken for themselves a second rate identity as the 'adopted' children of God, and a spiritual apartheid has developed between Christ and Christians. Although this identity given to Jesus has served as a spiritual matrix for Christians, in which they find security, protection and nourishment, this matrix can become a prison if people are kept in it beyond their need. Now the time has come for Christianity to grow out of this system and liberate itself from spiritual slavery.

The Christian tradition is in the process of growing. We can accept the elevation of Jesus and have the humility to accept that we are still far from the goal of fully understanding the person and message of Christ. The early church could only understand Jesus in the way that it could in its time, and it was considered progressive. But we can also accept that it is not the ultimate way of understanding for it has built this wall between Christ and his followers.

Our task is to find the ultimate answer to Jesus' question, the answer that breaks down walls, bridges gulfs and creates communion between Christ and Christians, between God and all human beings. In fact Jesus himself gives the answer for every human being. He was born in the tradition of Abraham, as the son of Abraham, but he grew out of this and realized himself as the Son of God. He could say, 'Before Abraham was I am.'[107] He had to renounce his spiritual father and mother, his spiritual brothers and sisters, his spiritual wife and children, and enter into the kingdom of God to realize his real and eternal identity, the Son of God. The son of Abraham is included in the Son of God but he is transcended, but, on the other hand, the son of Abraham does not include the Son of God. The son of Abraham gives continuity to the past, but the Son of God or Daughter of God manifests eternity. The son of Abraham divides humanity but the Son of God unites humanity. If God had asked Jesus, 'Who do people say that I am?' Jesus might have replied, 'People say that you are the God of Abraham, the

God of Isaac and the God of Jacob.' Then God might have asked him, 'But who do you say that I am?' In this case Jesus might have replied solemnly, 'You are my beloved Father. You and I are ultimately one.' In giving this answer Jesus would free God from just being the God of Abraham, the God of Isaac and the God of Jacob and elevate him to be the God of all humanity, and the whole of creation.

Jesus' answer came from his direct encounter with God, but he was not able to tell people who he was, for his experience was not within the memory of his Jewish tradition, and he did not have adequate words with which to explain himself. Using different words, God might have told him, 'Blessed are you, for it is I who revealed this truth to you. This is the key to the kingdom of heaven that I have given to you, so that you may make it clear to all those who still think of God as just the God of Abraham, the God of Isaac and the God of Jacob, that God is the God and the Father of the whole of humanity and of creation.' Jesus then might have asked God, 'Who do people say that I am?' and God might then have answered, 'People say you are a son of Abraham, a son of Isaac, a son of Jacob and a son of David, son of Joseph or son of Mary.' If Jesus had asked him, 'But who do *you* say that I am?' God would have answered, 'You are my beloved Son, You and I are one.' Then Jesus would have rejoiced in the Holy Spirit saying, 'Father, Lord of heaven and earth, I thank you because you have hidden this mystery from the wise and understanding, but have revealed it to the simple. Yes Father, this is how you wanted it to happen.'[108]

Jesus realized for the first time who God is and who humanity is, and his 'I' became all humanity and all creation. Jesus did not reject or deny the Jewish memory but he made it his own discovery and transcended it. God is not just the God of

Abraham or the God of the Jews, but he is the God of all humanity and the whole of creation. God gave his ultimate answer to Jesus and Jesus, representing the whole of humanity and creation, gave the ultimate answer to God and broke down the walls between God and humanity.

Jesus asks every one of his disciples the same question. He says, 'Who do people say that I am?' We might reply, 'People say that you are John the Baptist. Some say you are the prophet Elijah, some others say you are the prophet Jeremiah, some others say that you are one of the old prophets returned.' But Jesus will then ask, 'Who do you say that I am,' a question which implies, 'Who are you?' To ask who Jesus is, is to ask who we are. If our answer to Christ is, 'You are the Christ, the Son of God,' we are saying, 'I am a Christian, a follower of Christ. I am an adopted son or daughter of God. My God is the Father of Jesus Christ.' With this one is just moving from a relationship with the God of Abraham into a relationship with God who is the father of Jesus Christ. But just as Jesus grew from the tradition of the God of Abraham into the heart of God as his father, so now Christians have to grow from the tradition of the God of Jesus Christ into the heart of God as their father or mother, and finally to be able to say 'I and the Father are one.'

As we have seen, the memory of tradition can be thought of as a mother in whose womb one needs to be nourished and carried for it gives security, nourishment and protection. But when the time is ready everyone has to leave the womb of his or her spiritual mother and see the light of the sun for the first time. But the Christian, or at least the Catholic, tradition has become a mother who wants to conceive but who does not want to give birth. Her womb is open for conception but closed for delivery. Such a mother who does not want to give birth kills her children in the womb without giving them the chance of seeing the light of the sun. It is terrifying to see what Christianity is doing in the name of Christ. Christianity has closed her womb and refuses to accept that any of her children can be freed from her motherly protection, at least until their deaths. Christianity needs to repent, open her womb to her children and free them from the memory of Jesus Christ so that they can have the same experience of Jesus in the original way.

Like the God of Abraham, the God of Jesus Christ, as experienced by the followers of Jesus, divides humanity into those who believe in and worship Jesus Christ and those who do not worship Jesus Christ. Only the God who is each person's father and mother can unite all creation and all of humanity. The Son or Daughter of God is not one individual but the whole of humanity and the whole of creation. In this sense God has only one son or daughter, the whole of his or her creation. When God says to a person, 'You are my beloved son or daughter,' he is not referring to one particular individual but to the whole of humanity. A daughter has to grow into a Daughter of God and a son has to grow into a Son of God. If we were to ask God, 'Who do you say that I am,' God will surely reply, 'You are my beloved Son or my beloved Daughter, I and you are one,' and we can encounter the God, who says, '*I am who I am*,' the God of eternity. In this way the God of memory is *made a present reality*. We no longer see God with the spectacles of the past, but we see God with our own eyes.

Eternal life is not the repetition of the past, and cannot be repeated into the future. It is ever original, unique and unrepeatable, so that the 'present' of the human consciousness becomes a pure mirror in which the eternal reflects in all its splendor; the present and the eternal merge into one. Just as water falls from the sky onto the water below and becomes one with it, so eternity and time become one. The heavenly '*I am*' and the earthly 'I am' become one. Heaven and the earth become one. The eternal '*I am*' says to the present 'I am', 'You are my beloved son' or 'You are my beloved daughter, I and you are one.' The present 'I am' calls the eternal '*I am*' '*Abba, Father, Amma, Mother.*' This is the experience of the kingdom of God.

Chapter **13**

The Virgin, the child and the wise men

To be a virgin spiritually is to be free from the God of memory and in this sense a virgin can give birth to the God of eternity. A virgin who conceives with the help of a man gives birth to the past, to the memory and to continuity, whereas a virgin who gives birth without the help of a man, transcends time and conceives from eternity giving birth to the Son or Daughter of God, Emmanuel, God with us.[109] Only a virgin can conceive the saviour of the world who will free humanity from the past. Such a Son or Daughter of God remains a virgin for all time in the internal sense that he or she will neither be a descendant nor give rise to descendants; he or she is without a past, without a future, without a father and without a child. Symbolically it is significant that Jesus was born of a virgin without a human father representing the past, and that he remained a virgin leaving no descendants to give continuity to the past. In the physical sense a virgin is one who is innocent, ignorant and unconditioned by sexual experience. Psychologically and spiritually, a virgin is one who stops the historical progression of the God of memory and opens herself to the living reality of the God of eternity. As long as we give continuity to the God of memory within our consciousness we are not virgins and we are unable to give birth to the God of eternity.

A child is one who has not been conditioned by experience. A newborn child has no name, no language, no religion and no culture, and with his or her unconditioned mind is open to all possibilities. In this sense a child is also a virgin. As it grows it is conditioned and as it acquires a name, a language, a religion and a culture the virginity and the unconditioned mind are lost. Jesus said that one has to become like a child, which means one has to free oneself from the conditioning of life and realize one's original innocence and purity. Whereas a newborn child is both ignorant and innocent, a person who has become like a child is wise and innocent.

A wise person is not one who accumulates knowledge and who knows all the scriptures, but one who has realized the limitation of all knowledge and all scriptures and who looks into the sky of eternity for the appearance of wisdom. A wise person is one who reaches the boundary or limit of his or her own religion and realizes the relativity of these boundaries.

> When they saw the star, they rejoiced exceedingly with great joy, and going into the house they saw the child with Mary his mother and they fell down and worshipped him. When they had opened their treasures they offered him gifts, gold, frankincense and myrrh.'[110]

There are two ways of living – the creative way and the mechanical way. The nature of God is creative and God created humanity to live a creative life. But humanity falls from this creative life into the mechanical life that comes from the mind, from memory, and from knowledge. Creative life, on the other hand, comes from the spirit that is beyond the mind, memory and knowledge. Mechanical life moves horizontally whereas creative life unfolds vertically – but they are not independent for the creative life does use the horizontal dimension. Spirit is the master and the mind is the vehicle. Sin changes these roles so that the mind leads the spirit, the vehicle leads the master.

> *Creative life is a life of wisdom whereas mechanical life grows out of knowledge.*
>
> *Wisdom can use knowledge but knowledge cannot use wisdom.*
>
> *Wisdom is born from above; knowledge is the accumulation of the past.*
>
> *Wisdom is like the flowing river; knowledge is like a pot of water separated from the living river.*
>
> *Wisdom is alive; knowledge is dead.*
>
> *Wisdom is quality; knowledge is quantity.*
>
> *Wisdom cannot be seen with the naked eye but can be perceived by the heart.*
>
> *Wisdom is as light as a feather or as invisible as the wind, but knowledge is heavy with the accumulation of years.*
>
> *Knowledge burdens but wisdom frees one from the burden of knowledge. Wisdom gives life to dead knowledge. It is like pouring a pot of water into the river again, or the river flowing into stagnant water.*
>
> *To acquire knowledge one needs money and time, but wisdom is given freely, Wisdom can satisfy our desire for truth but knowledge cannot.* ·
>
> *Wisdom is as simple as milk and as eternal as wine.*
>
> *Wisdom does not grow old; it is always one day old.*
>
> *Wisdom is as old as creation and as young as a newborn babe.* ·

Wisdom is born of a virgin mind, in which the power of knowledge is silenced. Mary represents the virgin mind, and the child Jesus represents the eternal wisdom born from God. The child is the symbol of the creative life. The birth of wisdom is a great joy for those who are waiting for it and who want to place themselves under its guidance. But those who want to give continuity to their accumulations from the past find wisdom a threat because it puts an end to each independent movement of the past, whether it is political, religious or spiritual.

The wise men were seekers of God and seekers of truth. As philosophers they had discovered the limitations of their minds in their quest to understand the truth. Wisdom manifests herself to the virgin mind that has relaxed the movement of knowledge and has looked into the sky of eternity for wisdom to appear for its guidance. In this psychological or spiritual sense the wise men were virgins, relaxing their minds and looking up to the sky for the star, for wisdom, to manifest. When Mary, the virgin *par excellence* gave birth to the wisdom *par excellence*, the star appeared in the sky. The wise men saw that eternal wisdom had been born and they began their journey to meet the child.

> Behold wise men from the East came to Jerusalem saying, 'Where is he who has been born King of the Jews? For we have seen his star in the East and have come to worship him'.[111]

The star appeared in the East and it is in the East that the new day is born, where new life begins. The wise men who came from the East represent a mind in which ignorance has come to an end and in which the light of truth has appeared. The sun rises in the East and then sets in the West and this represents a journey, that is to say, time. But a star, eternity, guided this journey. The fulfillment of time is to be guided by eternity so that time is at the service of eternity. The fulfillment of knowledge is to be at the service of wisdom, to be a vehicle of wisdom. If time is cut off from eternity and goes on its own way it becomes a monstrous evil; knowledge cut off from wisdom becomes a burden to people.

Wisdom is seeing the extra-ordinary in the ordinary, and when the wise men saw the star in the sky it guided them to the child in the manger. They were old in body but they were children in mind, and although it could be that they were married and had children, they were virgins in their minds for they realized the limitations of their minds and their knowledge. The virgin minds of the wise men were led to the virgin worshiping the baby. Wisdom bridges the gap between the heaven and the earth, between the inside and the outside, between the ordinary and the extra-ordinary, between the child and the old man.

The star appears and disappears. When one leaves the security of the mind and knowledge, the star appears and guides. But when one falls back onto the mind the star disappears. To encounter the star, to encounter the wisdom, and to be led by it, is an experience of great joy. There are moments in one's life when the star appears clearly, at other times it disappears, for instance when doubts enter our minds, but then again it appears to cast out all these doubts. To be led by a star is an adventure.

> When they had heard the king they went on their way and lo, the star which they had seen in the East went before them till it came to rest over the place where the child was. And going into the house they saw the child with Mary his mother, and they fell down and worshiped him.[112]

The child with its mother is an archetypal symbol revealing the purpose and destiny of every human being in his or her spiritual journey. The search of the mind culminates in the encounter with the child born of a virgin. The search for knowledge comes to fulfillment when the mind discovers the wisdom born of God. We can see mother Mary as the whole human past, made virgin by relaxing the movement of continuity and giving birth from above, from God. A virgin becomes a mother and remains a virgin; this is the call of every human being, whether in marriage or in celibacy.

The wise men are symbols of human knowledge that has become virgin by falling at the feet of the child. 'And they fell down and worshiped him.' Knowledge is old, but wisdom has just been born. It is a beautiful scene in which knowledge falls at the feet of wisdom. Then the wise men offer everything they had accumulated during their search for truth. Opening their treasures they offered the baby gifts of gold, frankincense and myrrh. Again this is a beautiful representation of the culmination of the search of the human mind, which not only falls at the feet of wisdom but also offers all its possessions to wisdom to be used by wisdom. The mind can accumulate material, sensual or spiritual treasure. Gold represents material riches, myrrh represents sensual riches and incense represents spiritual riches. Nothing is rejected, everything is placed at the service of wisdom, and everything is consecrated, everything has found its proper and rightful place.

At the same time Herod wanted to kill the child. There are two kinds of seeker – the person who wants to find error and to kill, and the person who, with a pure heart and mind, is searching for the truth to worship it, as did the wise men. The first kind is closed, arrogant and defensive while the other is pure and humble. Herod represents established power structures, the mind that clings to power, that finds security in power and wants to continue that power from generation to generation. Any new idea, proposal, movement or charismatic person is seen as a threat. This kind of mind does not hesitate to use violence to protect itself and to ensure the continuation of its position and power. This kind of mind reduces truth to a system of knowledge to be protected. It sees itself as the guardian of the structure, and, always fearful, suspicious and defensive, seeks to protect the *status quo*.

Now when Jesus was born in Bethlehem of Judea in the days of Herod the King, behold wise men from the East came to Jerusalem saying, 'Where is he who has been born king of the Jews?' When Herod the king heard this he was troubled and all Jerusalem with him.[113]

Herod was troubled, he was afraid of the child because the child was a threat to his throne, and his power. He was quick to act, and 'assembling all the chief priests and scribes of the people, he inquired where the Christ was to be born.' He was astute and quickly got the information he needed. He did not respect the scriptures and rather than accept the plan of God, he acted against it. 'Go and search for the child and when you have found him bring me word that I too may come and worship him.'

A mind that is closed in on itself is dead, it is a mind that has defined the truth and which refuses life and wisdom. But it is not possible to kill wisdom just as a dead person cannot kill a living person. Herod was already dead because he had structured the truth and put it into the tomb of knowledge. Wisdom and knowledge cannot live together in the same house as equals. One is life and the other is death, one is master and the other is an instrument.

The wise men were warned in a dream not to return to Herod, so they left for their own country.'[114] Herod realized that the wise men had tricked him and in a rage, 'he sent and killed all the male children in Bethlehem and in all that region, who were two years old or under according to the time which he had ascertained from the wise men.' The mind that seeks power and continuity, including spiritual power and continuity, is blind and has no compassion; it becomes merciless and violent. Wisdom is a threat to power and continuity and has to be killed but she has her own way of defending herself:

> Now when they had departed, behold an angel of the Lord appeared to Joseph in a dream and said, 'Rise, take the child and his mother and flee to Egypt and remain there till I tell you; for Herod is about to search for the child to destroy him.'[115]

The wise men were the opposite of Herod, they were seekers after truth and were humble, open, waiting with patience to receive the wisdom as a pure gift, pure grace from above. They had nothing to defend, nothing to propagate, and all they did is to prostrate themselves at the feet of wisdom and to offer everything they had as a gift to the Gift that they had received, so everything became a gift. Only those who have received wisdom as a pure gift know how to offer their lives as a gift to the wisdom.

When a wise person desires his or her continuity then he or she becomes a Herod. It is rare for a wise person to become a Herod but it is possible for the disciples to transform him into a Herod. When a Herod renounces his desire for continuity then he or she becomes a wise person. At any time each one of us can become a Herod or a wise person.

The virgin, the child and the wise men at the feet of the child offering their gifts, is a wonderful symbol for our daily life. They are all symbols of the relaxation of the movement of continuity and the opening of life to eternal wisdom. The old is at the service of the new, the past is at the service of the present. Knowledge is at the service of wisdom, time is at the service of eternity. Usually it is the old who lead the child, the past that guides the present, and knowledge tries to define wisdom, time moves towards eternity. But here the roles are reversed. A newborn baby leads the old, the present guides the past and eternity manifests itself in time. This is the arrival of the kingdom of God.

Chapter 14

Preach the gospel to all creation

The Good News of the kingdom of God is the proclamation that God is everywhere, was everywhere and will be everywhere, and that each person should stop his or her movements and realize that he or she is already in God. The apostles were asked to go and proclaim this to all creation.

Before proclaiming the Good News Jesus had to discover it within himself, in his own life. This discovery took place at his baptism when the heavens opened and the Spirit of God came upon him and he realized that he was the Son of God. He discovered God was his Father, the foundation of his being. The heavens are of course always open and it is the human heart that has built walls and a roof separating itself from the light of heaven. When the walls and the roof are removed then the human heart finds itself under the light of the sun and knows its true identity in relationship to God.

Jesus was in the womb of Judaism, his spiritual mother. Jesus grew up with the God of Abraham, Isaac and Jacob and was protected and nourished by this. But when he was fully grown he realized that this womb could no longer contain him and at his baptism he forced himself out of the womb of his spiritual mother. For the first time he saw the light of God directly and discovered his real identity in relationship to God.

In Jesus humanity returned to its original state of being in the image and likeness of God. He did this by realizing himself, and the whole of humanity, as the Son or Daughter of God. Jesus not only realized that he was the Son of God, but also that he and God were one saying, 'I and the Father are one.' The Good News that God has proclaimed, the final revelation of God to humanity, is to discover that 'I am the son or daughter of God.'

It would be wrong to think that God announced this Good News to one individual, separate from all other individuals. For God announced it to every creature, not only men and women but to all sentient and non-sentient beings. By saying to Jesus, 'You are my beloved son,' God has proclaimed his Good News to the whole of creation. What greater news can there be than for a creature to hear from God, 'You are my beloved son,' or 'You are my beloved daughter,' or 'You are my beloved manifestation?' When Jesus heard the voice of the Father telling him that he was the beloved Son of God, he did not hear it for himself alone, he heard it for every creature. Jesus stood in the presence of God together with the whole of creation.

If God had proclaimed one individual to be his beloved son or daughter, he would not have been proclaiming good news. In doing this he would have been saying, 'You are privileged to be my beloved son or beloved daughter. Everyone else is condemned to being my adopted son or adopted daughter.' Likewise any individual person who hears only for himself or herself, 'You are my beloved son,' or 'You are my beloved daughter,' would turn and say, 'I am blessed to be the only beloved son of God or daughter of God and all of the rest of you are condemned to be the adopted sons and the adopted daughters of God, second-grade children.'

The Good News that Jesus heard in the cave of his heart is

announced and proclaimed by God to every creature, and so it became Jesus' mission to proclaim it to all creation. His message to humanity was, 'You are the son of God; you are the daughter of God; you are the manifestation of God. You are not aware of this, I want you to discover it and I want you to realize this eternal truth.' Jesus discovered that the foundation of his being was God, that the foundation of every created being is God, and that in a mysterious way creation is the manifestation of God. Actually this was not new, for God had revealed what humanity is from the beginning of creation, but humanity then had lost this awareness in the Garden of Eden.

Each one of us has two selves. The first is the phenomenal self, the ego, which has its origin in time and space. The second is the eternal self, which has its origin from above, from God. One is born of flesh and blood; the other is born of the spirit. To discover that 'I am the son of God,' or 'I am the daughter of God,' is to discover that eternal self which is in each one of us and which has its origin in God. It is the eternal self which says, 'I am the image and likeness of God,' or 'I am the son of God or daughter of God,' and it is even possible for this eternal self to enter the bosom of God and say, 'I and God are one.'

Jesus said, 'I am the light of the world,'[116] and 'You are the light of the world.'[117] These two statements are different sides of the same coin, for when Jesus discovered that the foundation of his being, God, was the light of the world, he also discovered that the foundation of every being and every created being, which is God, was also the light of the world. These two statements are like two wheels of a cart and to proclaim the Good News one has to proclaim both at the same time. Unfortunately Christianity has concentrated on 'I am the light of the world,' and has neglected 'You are the light of the world,' the statement that Jesus addressed to the whole of humanity. We have been dragging the one-wheeled cart of Christianity in such a way that the burden has fallen completely on the side without the wheel, that is, on humanity. In this way Christianity has become a tremendous burden and Christ, who came to remove all burdens from the human heart, has himself become a tremendous burden. Christ, who came to free people from slavery, has been transformed into cords that bind people.

Jesus did not say you *must become* the light of the world or the salt of the earth[118] but he said you *are* (already) the salt of the earth, but you have lost this awareness and I want you to discover it. When Jesus said, 'I am the light of the world,' he stopped the movement of time, the movement of desire, the movement of becoming and the movement of history, and he initiated the movement of eternity, the movement of unfolding. In him the world of time has come to an end, for although he had a functional future in which to fulfill his mission, he had no psychological future in which he had to *become* something else. When he proclaimed to humanity, 'You are the light of the world,' he was telling humanity to stop this movement of desire and the movement of time and realize that it *is already* the light of the world. In this sense he announced the end of the world, which is the end of psychological time, the end of desire and the end of becoming. By telling people that they have to *become* the light of the world or the salt of the earth we are placing a heavy burden on their shoulders, whereas Jesus came to take away all burdens and give people rest.

> Come to me all you who labor and who are heavy laden. I will give you rest. Take my yoke upon you, and learn from me, for I am gentle and lowly in heart and you will find rest for your souls. For my yoke is easy and my burden is light.[119]

Jesus did not *become* the Son of God but discovered that he *was already* the Son of God. He did not become the light of the world, but discovered that he was already the light of the world. By realizing who he was, Jesus was freed from the burden of becoming and from all artificial ideals of perfection. He also realized that people were carrying heavy burdens in the name of God and religion and he felt compassion for them. He invited people to discover their real identity in which they can be free from all burdens and find inner rest in their lives, just as Jesus had found inner rest by realizing who he already was. The yoke of Jesus is not really a yoke rather it takes away all yokes. The cross of Jesus is not a burden to be carried rather it takes away all crosses. His way is easy and light since there is no burden of becoming. So the whole of the Good News of Jesus is in these two statements, 'I am the light of the world', and 'You are the light of the world'.

Scientific research seeks to discover the foundation of matter on which the universe is built. Scientists have discovered that the atom, which they had thought was solid matter, is not really solid matter but is energy. The material universe we can see is the solidification of energy and it is now clear that matter and energy are different manifestations of the same thing. There are not two different realities but matter appears as energy and energy appears as matter. In the same way Jesus discovered that the foundation of human consciousness is God, that he is the expression of the Father and that they are one and the same. When Jesus said, 'I and the Father are one,' he was not describing two realities, he and God, but the fact that there is only one God and he was God's manifestation. So God and creation are not two separate realities – God is the only reality and creation is the manifestation of God. If God is the eternal

'Word', the creation is the 'word' in time and space and every creature is a 'word' of God. This is the Good News; this is the eternal truth.

To discover this we need a pure mind and a loving and compassionate heart. The interior path is the only way to discover this news for ourselves and for the whole of creation. We have to seek the foundation of our being just as scientists seek the foundation of the material universe. This journey is a journey on which we must die to all identities, every conclusion, every belief, which separates us from God and which creates a reality outside God. We have to die to all identities that separate us from one another and from the created world. We have to die continually within ourselves until we discover that we are united with every created being and with God, and always have been. When he said, 'Unless a grain of wheat falls to the ground and dies, it remains alone, but when it dies it gives a mighty harvest.'[120] Jesus was talking of the way of interior death.

Only when we die to everything that separates us from others and from God can we hear the Good News of God, 'You are my beloved son', or 'You are my beloved daughter', or 'You are my beloved manifestation'. We then can have the courage to call God, '*Abba*, Father', or '*Amma*, Mother'; but this call is made on behalf of all creation. The consciousness which calls God '*Abba*, Father' is not a particular individual consciousness but a universal consciousness in which the whole of creation and the whole of humanity is present, from the beginning to the end of creation. With this realization one's mission in life is to go and proclaim this Good News to every creature.

A Sufi master once said, 'When I look outside I find myself as a bubble in the ocean. But when I look inside I find the whole universe as a bubble within me.' The foundation of our being is so great and profound that it can and does contain the whole universe. The whole of creation is in God and if God is in us, then the whole of creation is in each one of us. Externally we cannot reach the end of the world or reach out to every creature. Externally we cannot announce the Good News to those who have died before the coming of Christ and to all those who have not heard the gospel. But the fulfillment of our lives does not depend on external achievements. Jesus did not have external success, he did not announce to the whole of the world in an external sense. What he did externally was very little and, externally, his life ended in failure, but what he achieved internally is infinite and eternal.

Internally Jesus went to the whole world and announced the Good News to the whole of creation. He saw every creature as the manifestation of God, and in a way he saw the salvation of every human being and every creature, for salvation is nothing more than the discovery that each one of us is the manifestation of God. This is not something that we can achieve through effort but is a pure gift of God given from all eternity and our response is to discover it. Imagine a son who, after the death of his father, found his father's last will and the place in which his father had hidden his treasure. It is good news for the son but he has to go and dig until he finds the treasure. God is the treasure hidden in the heart of every creature, and Jesus calls to every individual to dig and discover this infinite treasure, the foundation of our being, the kingdom of God.

This internal journey is not an individual egotistical journey but a journey in which every creature participates because each one of us is connected to every other person and every creature. There is no individual discovery in relation to God; every discovery of God is universal. Unless one's individual consciousness grows into universal consciousness one cannot hear the voice of God for the whole of creation. When one finds the kingdom of God one finds it for the whole of humanity and must proclaim it and share it with others. One must announce, 'I have discovered that the kingdom of God is hidden in our hearts,' or it may be more skillful to say, 'I have discovered we are in God but unaware of it. We are living in God, we are moving in God and have our beings in God, just as a fish lives in the ocean but is not aware that it is in the ocean.' This Good News can only be announced, it cannot be preached, and it is every person's responsibility to search for it and to find it. Religions can help men and women discover this hidden treasure, but what we need so much today is not believers in God but seekers of God. Belief is only the beginning of our search.

Then Jesus said, 'He who believes and is baptized will be saved and he who does not believe will be condemned.'[121] To live without knowing our inner treasure, who is God, is to live in ignorance, to live a life of death. But to live our life knowing our hidden treasure is the life of salvation. To live without knowing who we are is death, but to live knowing who we are is the life of salvation. To discover this reality we must either believe the Good News that the kingdom of God is buried within us or at least have a desire to find the foundation of our being.

The fulfillment of life is finding the kingdom of God. Once he had discovered the kingdom for himself and for the whole of creation, Jesus was able to say, 'First you seek the kingdom and its righteousness and all things will be added unto you.'[122] He invited his disciples to first of all find this kingdom within themselves and then to go out to the world and invite people to discover that they are already in the kingdom of God. The kingdom of God is not the goal of spiritual life for we are already in it, rather the purpose of spiritual life is to 'repent' that is to stop all movement of desire and becoming and see that God is everywhere.

Chapter 15

Creative life and prayer

As we have seen, life can either be creative or it can be mechanical. Mechanical life is a life of repetition, fixed and inflexible, in which there is only imitation, the past entering into the present and the present projecting itself into the future. In a mechanical life what was, what is and what will be, are one and the same (although there may be some minor changes here and there). This type of life cannot be called 'Life' and although one may live for a hundred years one may have no more than one day's experience. Creative or original life cannot be defined, for the moment we define creative life it becomes mechanical. It can only be described in negative terms; it is not mechanical, it is not a repetition of the past. The life of Jesus is a perfect example of a creative life, full of creative responses to real situations.

The Scribes and the Pharisees wanted to catch Jesus out so they asked him some trick questions. The question, 'Is it lawful to pay taxes to Caesar?'[123] was cunningly designed to trap Jesus, for if he had replied that it was lawful to pay taxes to Caesar they could have accused him of being an enemy of the Jews because he was asking them to obey the emperor and be subject to him. If on the other hand he had replied that it was unlawful to pay taxes to Caesar then they could have accused him of being an

enemy of the emperor. Either answer would have been danger-
ous. But Jesus replied, 'Give to Caesar what is Caesar's and give
to God what is God's.' This was not a mechanical answer from
the past, it was not in the collective memory of humanity, and
no one had given such an answer before. Jesus gave an original
and creative answer, appropriate to that particular situation. It
clearly had an impact on the Scribes and the Pharisees who were
'amazed and did not dare ask any more questions'.

On another occasion the Scribes and the Pharisees brought
the woman caught in the act of adultery, and asked Jesus a similarly devious question. 'This woman is caught in the act of
adultery. Moses has commanded us to stone such people, what
do you say?'[124] If Jesus had told them not to stone the woman
to death they could have accused him of breaking the law of
Moses, whereas if he had told them to stone her then they
could have accused him of having no compassion as a man of
God. Both answers could have invited condemnation from the
Scribes and the Pharisees. But Jesus replied, 'Which of you is
without sin, let him throw the first stone.' The answer had a
powerful impact and they all left, 'one after the other, beginning from the eldest to the youngest'. Jesus did not respond
from the past, from his mind; instead the response, immediate
and inspired, came from the spirit, from eternity. On the occasion when a rich young man asked Jesus a question, Jesus first
gave a response from the past:

> 'Teacher, what good deed must I do to have eternal life?' And he
> said to him, 'Why do you ask me about what is good? No one is
> good but God alone. If you would enter life keep the command-
> ments.' He said to him, 'Which?' and Jesus said, 'You shall not
> kill, you shall not commit adultery, you shall not steal, you shall
> not bear false witness. Honor your father and mother.[125]

All Hebrews knew these commandments so this answer was not original or creative, in that Jesus repeated something from the past. But when this young man said to Jesus, 'All these I have observed, what do I still lack?' Jesus followed up with a fully creative answer, 'If you would be perfect, go sell what you possess and give to the poor, and you will have treasure in heaven, and come and follow me.' This answer was not from the memory, or the mind, but from the spirit, the creative source beyond the mind. Jesus invited everyone to enter the creative life, which he called the life of the Kingdom of God by being 'reborn'. He said to Nicodemus:

> Truly, truly I say to you unless one is born anew, he cannot see the kingdom of God... truly, truly I say to you that unless one is born of water and Spirit, he cannot enter the kingdom of God. That which is born of the flesh is flesh, and that which is born of the Spirit is spirit.[126]

The term 'flesh' refers both to the physical body and to the spiritual life lived before the arrival of Christ, the life lived according to the law, 'for the law was given to Moses, grace and truth came through Jesus Christ.'[127] Life lived according to the law is mechanical, it is a life in which the past enters the present and the present goes into the future. But to all who received him, who believed in his name, he gave the power to become children of God, who were born, 'not of blood nor of the will of the flesh nor of the will of man, but of God.'[128]

To be born of the flesh, to be born of blood, to be born of the will of man, all signify birth into the mechanical life. To be born of the flesh is to live in the movement in time, the transmission of the past into the present and the present into the future, and is characteristic of our psychological and spiritual life as well as physical life. The spiritual flesh is the life lived before the coming of Christ that was passed on from generation to generation as the spiritual tradition of the patriarchs and the law of Moses. Living in the flesh we not only give continuity to our physical bodies but also to our psychic and spiritual bodies, our spiritual experiences and spiritual convictions.

To be born from above, to be born of the Spirit, to be born from God, is to be born into the creative life. This is a life that comes from God, a life in which time relaxes and eternity manifests. This type of life is one in which there is no entry of the past into the present, no projection of the present into the future, but is a life which comes from eternity. Jesus describes this life of rebirth to Nicodemus:

> That which is born of the flesh is flesh and that which is born of the Spirit is spirit. Do not marvel that I said to you, 'You must be born anew,' the wind blows where it wills and you hear the sound of it, but you do not know whence it comes or whither it goes; so it is with everyone who is born of the Spirit.[129]

In the life of the Spirit there is no movement of time, it is like the wind; nobody knows from whence it comes and nobody knows where it goes. It has no past and no future; it was not in the past, it will not be repeated in the future. Humanity has developed many approaches and techniques to relax the movement of time, the movement of the ego, the movement of becoming, so that we can enter into the state of creativity. Rituals, dance, music, prayer and meditation have all been used to silence the mind. The essence of prayer is the relaxation of the movement of the ego, the movement of the flesh and blood, the movement of the will, the movement of psychological time and that horizontal movement that takes the past into the present and the present into the future. Jesus told us how to do it. He had the experience of the Spirit while he was praying at his baptism, a prayer so intense that it caused the heavens to open. Jesus summarized the essence of that prayer in one sentence, 'Thy will be done.' The prayer of Jesus was simple and direct. 'Not as I will but what you want.'[130] With the words 'not as I will,' Jesus relaxed the movement of the 'I', the movement of time and the past. He never projected the past into the future. With the words, 'as you want', he invited the movement of the Spirit, which comes from eternity. This prayer, the essence of unconditional surrender, was always on the lips of Jesus.

It is not easy for us to come to that state of prayer. Our 'I' has to go through a process of purification in relationship with God. We can visualize five different levels of prayer, or five ways in which the ego relates with God, as buildings with different roofs – the roof of stone, the roof of wood, the roof of wood with a window, the roof of glass and as a building without a roof. Above the roof is God, the ever-radiating sun.

When our ego is like a house with a stone roof, the sun cannot enter the house, and we live a life in which God is transcendent, far away from us. We may even doubt the existence of God. At this level our relationship with God is like that of a master and his servant and we pray to God for our needs just as a servant pleads with his master. We try to please God through prayers and sacrifices. As we grow in our prayer life and in our relationship with God, our 'I' can feel the presence of God as less transcendent, but at this level God treats us as friends rather than as servants. As we grow deeper into a life of prayer we can imagine that our roof is a roof of wood pierced with windows; some parts of the roof are dense, but other parts are clear glass. At this level of our relationship with God we see the light of the sun entering into us and we can experience God as both within us and at the same time as outside us. Our relationship with God is more like that of lovers and we can say, 'I love God as my beloved and God loves me as his lover.' There is intimacy and communion, but at this level there is also duality and a separation between God and us.

As our ego grows in its prayer life and in its relationship with God, the roof of wood is transformed into a roof of glass. Here the light of the sun passes through the glass without difficulty and the glass appears like the sun. The 'I' can feel that it is the sun, it is God, and we can identify ourselves with God, and our relationship with God is like a mystical marriage in which the lover and the beloved consummate their love. But at this level there is still a subtle 'I' and a mystical marriage cannot be the final level of experience.

At the level of the building without the roof (which can't really be called a level) there is no ego, no 'I', the roof disappears and only the sun remains. This experience can be called an 'awakening' or a 'breakthrough'. With this awakening, this penetration, the experiences that we have passed through in our four 'levels' appear as a dream. This is the level at which a person discovers his or her ontological oneness with God and can say, 'I and God are one.' Of course a person does not remain in the non-duality but comes down into functional duality in which there is, at least in a functional sense, a separation between the human being and God. This is the level in which one can say, 'Not as I will, but as you will.' At this level a person will know that to desire one's own will is to create an ego, to create a roof, and to become separate from God. So, a person has to say each moment of his or her life, 'God, thy will be done.' The ego accepts that God alone is the ultimate reality; it has no choice for it is a choice-less choice. When the ego is completely silent creativity manifests itself, and it is then that the kingdom of God arrives.

God created humanity to live a creative life and in restoring this original state to men and women, Jesus invited humanity to re-enter the creative life through spiritual rebirth or repentance. A life of prayer is one of the surest ways to reach this rebirth.

Chapter 16

The Abba experience of Jesus

At the center of Jesus' experience of God was the realization that human beings are greater than religion. He experienced God as '*Abba*' and asked his disciples to call God, '*Abba*' or Father as well. This *Abba* experience of Jesus was a revolution in, and the fulfillment of, the Jewish experience of God. It was a revolution because it marked a transition from spirituality centered on religion to spirituality centered on the human being. It was fulfillment because it was the inauguration of the new covenant that had been promised by God through the prophets, the covenant in which God was to write the law in the hearts of human beings.

Jesus realized that God was his *Abba*, his source and his foundation and that be could not exist without his Father. For Jesus, the expression 'Father' was not limited to the masculine aspect of God but reflected God as the source and foundation of his being. God was his father in the sense that he had come from God, but God was also his mother in the sense that he had originated from the eternal womb of God. The *Abba* experience of Jesus made him realize that God was not only a being but that God was love.

We can understand the *Abba* experience of Jesus in the context of four important moments in his life. The first was his birth as a human being. Mary, his physical mother conceived him, nourished him, gave him protection within her for nine months and then gave birth to him as a human being. The second was his birth as a Jew. The temple is a symbol of the spiritual womb and mother and on the eighth day Jesus was presented in the temple to be circumcised. Judaism then conceived him, nourished him, gave him spiritual protection for nine spiritual months, and gave birth to him into the universal womb of God. The third important moment was his baptism which was when he came out of the limited womb of his Jewish tradition, the womb of the God of Abraham, Isaac and Jacob, and entered into the eternal womb of God, the God who said, 'I am who I am'. Jesus the Jew was transcended and Jesus the Son of God was born when God said, 'You are my beloved son'. Jesus went beyond even this experience to realize that he and his Father were one and the fourth important moment was the discovery of his ontological identity with God at which point he was able to say, 'My Father and I are one'. Jesus the Son of God was transcended and Jesus the God was born. In this way we can see four stages in the life of Jesus. The first was Jesus as a human being, followed by Jesus as a Jew, then Jesus as the Son of God, and finally, Jesus the God. The first two stages relate to the origin of Jesus in space and time, while the second two relate to his origin in eternity.

With this understanding we can deepen our understanding of the *Abba* experience of Jesus, which, although a single experience, had many different aspects. In the Jewish spiritual tradition God was seen as creator and human beings were seen as creatures, the created. Philosophically the prophetic religions of Judaism, Christianity and Islam all believe that God created the world out of nothing. But thinking that God gave human beings existence, before which they were non-existent, creates a gulf between God and human beings, that can never be bridged, for even in heaven human beings remain as creatures. This view of the relationship between God and humanity satisfies many people, but it is oppressive in that it creates a spiritual apartheid between God and human beings. The *Abba* experience of God in which Jesus experienced God as Father, rather than as creator, abolished this spiritual apartheid. In his *Abba* experience Jesus broke down the dividing wall between God and creatures and established a new heaven (God) and a new earth (creation). He then announced this Good News to humanity, saying, 'My brothers and sisters, you are not creatures of God but sons and daughters of God. You are not created out of nothing but you came from the eternal womb of God and have the choice-less choice to return to the womb of God. God is not our creator but our Father.'

The *Abba* experience of Jesus revealed God as the Father of humanity and the whole of creation. The God of the Jewish tradition divided humanity into Jews and Gentiles, the chosen people and the people who had not been chosen. At his baptism Jesus came out of the womb of the God of Abraham and experienced God as the Father of all. God cannot be the private property of any one person or any one religion and in his *Abba* experience of God Jesus liberated God from being the God of just the Jews. He broke down the barrier and created one God and one humanity, in which both Jews and Gentiles become the chosen people of God.

In his *Abba* experience of God Jesus realized that God was the foundation of his being. This experience can be likened to a tree that in the beginning imagines itself as independent of the earth, and even doubts the existence of the earth. Then the

tree discovers the earth and discovers that it is totally dependent on the earth and cannot exist, even for a moment, without
the support of the earth.

The *Abba* experience of Jesus was the inauguration of the
new covenant, which God had promised through the prophets.
In the old covenant of the Ten Commandments God had told
human beings what they should do and what they should not
do. The new covenant revealed to people who they *are* rather
than what they should *do*. When Jesus had the experience of
the Spirit, God did not give him any commandments as he had
done to Moses, rather he told Jesus, 'You *are* my beloved Son'.
With these words he wrote the law in the heart of Jesus and in
the hearts of all people.

In the *Abba* experience, Jesus realized that there was no
'way' to God. God is like an infinite ocean and we are all like
fish in the ocean, searching for the ocean not knowing that we
are already in the ocean. God is everywhere, just as the ocean
is to the fish, and we discover we are already in God only by
repenting, stopping all our movements.

The *Abba* experience of Jesus changed the role of religion in
the spiritual journeys of men and women and he opened the
cage of religion with the keys of the kingdom of Heaven so that
men and women could fly in the infinite sky of the kingdom of
God.

The *Abba* experience made Jesus realize that human beings
had the potential to walk on their own feet. He saw that religion had paralyzed humanity and was carrying it on a pallet,
rather than helping it walk on its feet. When people brought a
paralyzed man to Jesus on a pallet, Jesus looked at him and said,
'Get up, take up your pallet and walk.' The paralyzed man was
a symbol of paralyzed humanity being carried on the pallet of

religion. Jesus was saying, 'My brothers and sisters, you have the power to walk on your own feet. So far you have been carried on the pallet of religion, now get up, take the religion into your own hands and walk.'

From his *Abba* experience of God Jesus was able to say, 'I am the way, the truth and the life. Nobody comes to the Father except through me.' He had become an original person; he left the path of his fathers and no longer followed any way made in the past. He no longer had any model of life, nor any model person to imitate. He had no religion to which he belonged. He himself was the way, the truth and the life. Freed from the bur-den of the past Jesus walked lightly and invited people to his way of living in which every man and every woman can affirm, 'I am the way, the truth and the life.' There is no other way to come to this experience except the way through which Jesus came to it. This way is nothing but to come out of the womb of religion and enter into the universal presence of God. Jesus called this way 'repentence' or 'rebirth'. Truth is dynamic and manifests in living human beings, but the living nature of truth is not manifested in the static definitions of religion.

Within all these different aspects of the *Abba* experience of Jesus there is one central message; human beings are greater than religion. Religions are meant to serve human beings and human beings are not meant to serve religion. The Sabbath was made for man and not man for the Sabbath. Jesus showed this through his example when he washed the feet of his disciples. He came to serve and not be served. Religions should be at the service of their followers helping them realize their potential as the sons and daughters of God.

Chapter 17

A new vision of Christianity

For two thousand years Christianity has been preaching a God who said to Jesus, and only to Jesus, 'You are my beloved son,' thus creating a spiritual apartheid between God and creatures, between Christ and Christians. One natural Son of God and millions of people as adopted sons and daughters of God, second-grade children. But in the third millennium Christianity will proclaim a God who says to every human being in the depths of his or her heart, 'You are my beloved son', or 'You are my beloved daughter', and to every created being, 'You are my beloved manifestation'. In this way the spiritual apartheid that exists between Christ and Christians and between God and creation will be abolished and the whole of creation will be freed from its slavery, realizing itself as the manifestation of God.

For two thousand years Christianity, in the name of Good News, has been unwittingly proclaiming Jesus the oppressor who says, 'I have discovered that I am the only beloved Son of God and no human being in the world can have that experience. All are condemned to be my disciples and to worship me. They can only become the adopted sons and daughters of God.' But in the third millennium Christianity will proclaim Jesus the liberator who says, 'In the depths of my heart I have discovered that I am the beloved Son of God and in that experience I have also realized that every human being in the depths of his or her heart is a beloved son or a beloved daughter of God, and I want everyone to discover this.'

The self that discovers itself as the son or daughter of God is not the phenomenal self, the ego, but the eternal self in each one of us that is created in the image and likeness of God. When the phenomenal 'I' is renounced one discovers the 'I' of the son of God or the daughter of God. If one is bold enough to renounce even the 'I' of being the son of God or the daughter of God, one discovers the 'I' of God and can say, 'My real I is God – I am God'.

For two thousand years Christianity has been proclaiming Jesus as the light of the world and has neglected what Jesus also said to humanity, 'You are the light of the world'. In the third millennium Christianity will proclaim that not only is Jesus the light of the world but also that your deepest self, who is God, 'is the light of the world; discover it'.

For two thousand years Christianity has been preaching that there is no salvation outside Christ and outside the Church, although this attitude has changed now amongst some Christians. In the third millennium Christianity will proclaim that there is no one outside Christ and there is no one outside the Church. Christ and the Church are like a tree in which the whole of humanity is present. Every person from the beginning of creation to the end of time is in Christ and in the Church and all one has to do is to realize it. The consciousness of each person has to grow from its identification as a leaf of the tree to being part of the branch of the tree, then to being the stem and ultimately to being one with the roots of the tree. It is at that point that one realizes that every person and everything is in

Christ and in the church.

Christianity is not a theological system separated from other systems. A system is like a tomb, and only dead bodies go into tombs. Put Christianity into the tomb of a structure and you have a dead body. The body of Christ cannot be put into a tomb; it will rise and become universal, passing through walls in which the doors are closed. Christianity has no walls and no roof, for its roof is the infinite sky in which all systems are present.

Christianity manifests itself in structures only for the sake of those who imprison themselves unconsciously in such structures, so that they may ultimately be freed from the structure. For two thousand years Christianity has been teaching a Jesus who was killed physically, and who was put into a tomb guarded by soldiers, and that the body disappeared and Jesus received a body defying the laws of time and space. In the same way Christianity has killed Jesus spiritually by reducing his teaching to a set of dogmas. Christianity has put Jesus into an intellectual tomb and placed itself as guardian of the body so that nobody can steal it. But in the third millennium Christianity will proclaim that Jesus, the truth, has indeed been killed intellectually and put into an intellectual tomb, but that he has risen from the tomb and has become universal. He has risen and those who want to meet him should come out of their tombs and closed rooms.

For two thousand years Christianity has been teaching that Jesus came into the world to save, and that the mission of the church is to save souls. In the third millennium Christianity will proclaim that Jesus discovered the truth that God has saved every person from all eternity and proclaimed the unconditional love of God, inviting all men and women and all creation to discover this love for themselves. All God's actions are salvific. God has already saved what he has created. Creating and saving are not two different actions of God. Humanity has created its own bondage through ignorance and sin and now has to free itself and see that God has already saved it through unconditional love. Salvation is a free gift of God, the infinite treasure hidden in the heart of each person by the unconditional love of God. Salvation does not depend on human will, it is already there, buried in the human heart, although each person has the responsibility of finding it.

For two thousand years Christianity has been divided into denominations even to the extent of Christians killing each other. But in the third millennium all Christians will be united under the banner of one message, 'The kingdom of God is at hand, repent,' which means simply that the kingdom of God is everywhere, discover it for yourself, you are a manifestation of God, realize it. This is the Good News that Christians will discover and proclaim to all humanity. The only message that a Christian is asked to believe is 'seek and find'.

For two thousand years Christianity has been confined to the cages of creeds, beliefs and systems in which Christians are given nourishment, protection and security and from which they were forbidden to fly into the freedom of infinite space. But in the third millennium the cages of creed and belief will be transformed into nests in which Christians will be nourished and protected and given security until their wings are grown and they can fly into the infinite space of freedom, coming back to the nest from time to time for the celebration of the sabbatical rest and repose.

For two thousand years the keys of the kingdom of God that Jesus gave to Peter have been seen as the keys of power and authority to loosen and to bind, to close and to open the gates of heaven. But in the third millennium the keys that Jesus gave to Peter will no longer be seen as the keys that open and close the doors of heaven (for heaven has no doors), but they will be seen as the keys that liberate people from the prison of religion based on the law. During the time of Jesus, the law and the temple were made into absolutes that imprisoned people, but Jesus opened the gates of the prison with the keys of wisdom, and invited people to enter the new life of the kingdom of God. Only a mind that longs for power uses keys to imprison people and the keys of the kingdom of heaven can only be used to open gates and liberate people. This means making religion, the law and the temple into relative values and not absolute truths.

For two thousand years Christianity has been producing thousands of saints, martyrs, doctors, confessors and mystics, but has failed to produce one awakened person who has been able to stand on his or her own feet and proclaim, 'I am free'. In the third millennium Christianity will no longer produce saints, martyrs, doctors, confessors and mystics but will produce millions of awakened men and women who will discover their true being, and help millions of their sisters and brothers discover their own true being, and, standing on their own feet, declare, 'We are free'.

For two thousand years Christianity has been preaching that people cannot walk on their own feet and that we are all psychologically condemned to use crutches until we die. People who have tried to walk on their own two feet have been called unorthodox and condemned. But in the third millennium Christianity will proclaim that every man and woman has the potential to walk on his or her own feet during their own lifetime and that there is no need to wait until death to do away with the crutches of the law and religion. Crutches will be transformed into supports of the sort children use until they learn to walk. There will be great joy in the community whenever someone learns to walk by herself or himself, and it will be those who refuse to walk on their own feet who will be called unorthodox.

For two thousand years Christians have been called believers in Christ and believers in the kingdom of God. But in the third millennium Christians will no longer be called believers and will be called seekers of Christ and seekers of the kingdom of God. In this context one can reflect on the difference between a Christian and a *Christian*, between Christianity and *Christianity*. *Christianity* cannot be the beginning of one's spiritual life; it is the final and ultimate state of one's spiritual evolution in relationship to God. Christianity is only a nest in which Christians are nourished until their wings are grown. Christianity is an earthly mother while *Christianity* is a heavenly mother. The earthly mother conceives, gives protection in her womb, and when the time is ready gives birth to *Christianity*. A Christian is a bird growing in the nest, but a *Christian* is a bird that has fully grown and left the nest to fly into the freedom of infinite space.

Christ is a bird that was born into the nest of Judaism but at his baptism he left the nest and flew into the freedom of infinite space. There have been millions of Christians from the beginning of Christianity and there are more than a billion Christians today but a *Christian* has yet to be born, at least officially. Christianity has been conceiving for two thousand years, but has not yet given birth to one *Christian*, not because she cannot but because she has closed her womb and declared openly that nobody can escape from her womb while still alive.

Only after death can a person be free. When a mother opens her womb to conceive and then closes it so that she cannot give birth, then she transforms her womb into a tomb and becomes a devouring mother and a murderer, killing her children in the womb without them seeing the light of the sun. But if she opens her womb to give birth she becomes a life-giver. The greatness of Christianity is not to be found in how many people she has conceived in her maternal womb, but in how many children she has given birth to into the freedom of infinite space.

Every human being is essentially a Christian and is called to grow into a *Christian*. To grow into a *Christian* is the ultimate destiny of every human being born into this world. Christianity is organized as a religion, a structure, but *Christianity* cannot be organized as a structure. Entry into *Christianity* is an individual rather than a collective journey and each person has to leave Christianity to be born into *Christianity*. The purpose of Christianity is to conceive people as Christians and then to give birth to them as *Christians*. To become a *Christian* is to become a human being for the first time.

For two thousand years Christianity has been saying that when Christ was born wise men from the East left everything and came to worship the tiny baby, offering him gifts. But Herod saw the child as a threat to his power and his continuity. He tried to kill the child and in so doing killed many innocent children. Christianity has transformed itself into a Herod and has been killing every child it sees as a threat to her power and her continuity. She has become extremely suspicious of any creative idea and, like Herod, has become cunning and able to get information about those she sees as a threat and, again like Herod, is quick to take action.

When one desires continuity of power one becomes a

Herod, and when one renounces all desire for power and continuity one becomes a wise man or woman. A child is a threat to those who seek continuity, while every child is a blessing for those who seek discontinuity. Those who desire continuity kill every child before its birth, and those who desire discontinuity give life to every child that is born. But in every wise person there is a hidden Herod and in every Herod there is a hidden wise person. In the third millennium Christianity will renounce her desire for power, position and continuity, will transform herself into wise people, and leave her security in search of the child to lay all her accumulated riches at the feet of the child.

For two thousand years Christianity has been teaching the way of 'becoming perfect', without realizing that it is the desire to 'become' that was the cause of the fall of humanity from its original state of the life of unfolding. This life of becoming perfect has been a tremendous burden to people. In the third millennium Christianity will instead teach the way of 'unfolding' the life of God within us, the way of 'repentance', which is nothing other than silencing the movement of the ego, the desire to become. In the third millennium spirituality will concentrate on the negative way, the way of silencing the desire to become, as opposed to the positive way of striving for an ideal of perfection. This life of unfolding cannot be the goal or the aim of spiritual life, because it is something that happens spontaneously and naturally when one silences the movement of desire to become. Just as the fish in the ocean in its ignorance is searching for the ocean, so humanity will find help to stop its searching for God and find that it is already in God, and will find rest.

For two thousand years Christianity has been teaching a spirituality that divides God and creation. Spiritual men and women are asked to renounce the world for the sake of God, creating a duality between God and creation as if they were opposed to each other. Actually nobody can renounce the world because in a very real sense each person is dependent on the world until death. In the third millennium Christianity will no longer teach the spirituality of renunciation, except to renounce the view that God and creation are two opposing realities. Humanity will see that God and creation are an inseparable unity, like ice with water floating within it; the ice has a beginning and an end, just as creation has a beginning and an end as a manifestation of God.

When sages say that they renounce the world they do not mean that they renounce the material world, they mean renunciation of the artificial world of desire born through ignorance. The world is ruled by desire born of ignorance, and it is this desire that binds a person. So to renounce the *world* means to renounce the ignorance that created the desire to become, to possess and to acquire. The world is desire, and desire is born of ignorance so, in this sense, the world is ignorance. Ignorance binds one to the world and once it is renounced, one is free from the world and the world becomes a place of joy.

Desire to become binds one to the world; true wisdom of one's self frees one from this desire and enables one to see God in creation and creation in God. The desire to become plunges one into the unending ocean of no fulfillment and dissatisfaction; whereas knowing one's true nature transforms the ocean of desire into an ocean of joy and fulfillment in which life unfolds itself, just as the sun radiates its light. This is not monism nor is it pantheism, or panentheism.[131] This realization cannot be described by such concepts of the mind for the relationship between God and creation cannot be defined. Here the mind has to keep silent by saying, 'I don't know and I can't know'. The way in which God manifests this universe is beyond the comprehension of the human intellect.

For two thousand years Christianity has been teaching that only the Eucharist is the body and blood of Christ and that only the priest has the power to change the bread and the wine into the body and blood of Christ. In the third millennium Christianity will proclaim that the whole of the universe is the body and blood of Christ and that the whole universe is Christ and the Eucharist. Every human action is a eucharistic celebration in which men and women transform the spirit of God into his or her own flesh and give to his or her neighbor as a gift of grace and love. Just as a radio receives electromagnetic waves and transforms them into sound waves, so the human being receives the grace and love of God and transforms it, as a eucharistic act, into the action of love. Just as creating is the continuous eucharistic celebration of God in which the spirit of God is made into the material universe, so human action is also a eucharistic celebration.

For two thousand years Christianity has been following Jesus both on the road and in the boat, which separates it from direct contact with the ocean of God, and it has forgotten the call of Jesus to Peter to leave the boat and walk on the water and enter into direct contact with God. In the third millennium Christianity will appreciate the value of the road as a practical moral code, and the value of the boat as a belief structure, and will encourage its members to leave these and follow Jesus who walked on the water, and to imitate Peter, the first to follow the call of his master and walk on the water.

Following Jesus on the road and in the boat is the action of the ego. Following Jesus on the water is following through our being as the image and likeness of God. The ego cannot walk on the water; it is heavy and needs a vehicle. Only the image and likeness of God is as light as a feather and can walk on water. The image and likeness of God does not need a vehicle. To leave the boat and to walk on the water is to leave one's ego and discover in one's self the image and likeness of God in which there is a direct communion with God.

For two thousand years Christianity has been saying that Jesus is the only way to God and the only mediator between God and human beings, and that everyone is obliged to believe in Jesus to be saved. In the third millennium it will be said that Jesus is the only way to God in the sense that he has come to tell humanity that there is no 'way' to God and that God cannot be reached through ways and means. The fish in the ocean does not come to the ocean through ways or means, but only by renouncing all movement does it realize that it is already in the ocean. In the same way humanity comes to God when, realizing the futility of all ways, it finds that it has to renounce all ways.

Each one of these aspects of a renewed Christianity is full in itself. Understand one and one can understand all the others. What is being said about the renewal of Christianity is not new, for it is about the original state of human beings which will also be their final state as foretold by Jeremiah: 'I will put my law within them, and I will write it upon their hearts; and I will be their God, and they shall be my people. And no longer shall each man teach his neighbor and each his brother, saying, "Know the Lord, for they shall all know me." '[132] This 'new' covenant foretold by Jeremiah is none other than the 'original' or 'eternal' covenant written by God when he or she created humanity and which is the birthright of every human being.

The third millennium will be the year of the Lord's favor in which all things return to their original state. Christianity will again read the words of Isaiah that Jesus declared at the beginning of his ministry and will declare, as did Jesus on that occasion two thousand years ago, 'Today this scripture has been fulfilled in your hearing.'

> The Spirit of the Lord is upon me,
> Because he has anointed me to preach the good news to the poor,
> he has sent me to proclaim release to the captives
> and recovery of sight to the blind,
> to set at liberty those who are oppressed,
> to proclaim the acceptable year of the Lord.[133]

Part **4**

The Hindu-Christian experience of God

O my Soul what did you see?
O my soul, what did you see
When you reached the depths of my being?
I saw God in me
And I in God,
Yet He is outside of me
And I outside of Him.
I saw all people in me
And I in all people
Yet they are outside of me
And I am outside of them.
I saw the whole creation in me
And I in the whole creation
Yet the creation is outside of me
And I outside of the creation.
I saw all people living in God
And God living in all people
Yet God is outside of them.
I realized that my source is the Real
And I am only an appearance of it.
I found that the source of my being
Is beyond words and forms.

Chapter **18**

Non-duality in the Upanishads

At the heart of Indian spirituality is the experience of God as *advaita* or 'non-duality', which was expounded in the Upanishads, the culmination of the Indian search for truth, some 600 years before Christ. The Upanishads (literally to sit at the feet of a master) are teachings learnt by sitting at the feet of a master in the tradition of the guru communicating truth to the disciple, and are also called *Vedanta*. The Vedas are the Indian scriptures – the revealed truth, and *'anta'* means the end. So the *Vedanta*, the Upanishads, are the end of the search and the fulfillment of the Vedas. The Upanishads are the point at which the sages arrived at an understanding of God.

The sages, the *rishis* of the Upanishads, experienced four stages in their relationship with God as part of this search for truth. The first stage was the experience of God through nature, in the wonders of creation, and the communication of this discovery was through poetry, hymns and song. This stage in the development of the Vedas, known as the *Samhitas*, is full of poetry. The second stage of the relationship with God, known as *Brahmanas* was through rituals and sacrifice of which there was a wide variety in the Vedic period. Gradually the sages discovered that the mediation of their relationship with God through words and sacrifice meant that it was impossible to be close to God. Such mediation with God is like the yoke on bulls; the yoke unites the bulls but at the same time keeps them apart. So a third stage was arrived at in which the sages renounced hymns and sacrifices and 'entered the forest' to meditate within. This was a revolution in the human relationship with God, for it involved a journey from the known to the unknown, from security into insecurity. In the Christian tradition it is 'entering the dark night of the soul'. This stage is known as the *Aranyakas*. The fourth and final stage in the developing relationship with God was the stage in which humanity discovered that its true self is God; the true self and God are one and the same. With this experience the search came to an end for the sages had reached the end of their journey – *Vedanta*. This is the stage known as Upanishads.

The exterior journey that found God in nature and creation led the sages of the Upanishads to an interior search that started with the question, 'Who am I, what is my real self?' This search for the real self led them to identify four levels of consciousness, the waking consciousness, the dreaming consciousness, the deep sleep consciousness, and *Thuriya*, which literally means the fourth.

In coming to understand these levels of consciousness, and what they meant in terms of the search for God, the sages also came to explore the ideas of 'real', 'unreal', and 'illusion'. Real is that which exists in the past, the present and in the future – that which is real has no beginning and no end. Unreal is that which exists only in one time – either it was in the past or is in the present, or will be in the future. That which is unreal has beginning and end. Illusion is the opposite of real – it is that which was not, which is not and which will not be. The idea of a barren woman's child and the idea of a square circle are both contradictions, cannot exist and are examples of illusion. In their search for the true self, the sages of the Upanishads first became aware of waking consciousness, which is the awareness of our physical body and of objects outside of us and around us. They asked themselves whether this waking consciousness was real, unreal or illusion. They came to the conclusion that waking consciousness was not illusion because they were aware of it, that it was not real because it has a beginning and an end, and so waking consciousness had to be unreal.

The sages realized that when they went to sleep, the waking consciousness disappeared and they entered into the dreaming consciousness. So they asked themselves whether this dreaming consciousness was real, unreal or illusion. They came to the conclusion that it was not illusion because they were aware that it existed, that it could not be real because it disappeared upon waking or upon entering deep sleep, and so the state of dreaming consciousness was also seen to be unreal.

When the sages became aware of the deep sleep consciousness they asked the same questions and again concluded that it was not illusion as it existed, was not real because it was not permanent and so, again, deep sleep consciousness was seen to be unreal. At this point a breakthrough took place. The sages of the Upanishads had discovered that the real self was beyond all these levels of consciousness, and could only be experienced in the fourth state, which they called *Thuriya*. They called the real self experienced in this state, *Brahman, atman, tat, om, light, life reality* and the like. Once they had discovered this fourth state they communicated it through statements or utterances called *mahavakhyas*, or 'great sentences'. They were called great sentences because each one contained the whole truth so that if one *mahavakhya* is understood the whole truth, the whole experience of the Upanishads and the whole of reality, can be understood.

There are four *mahavakhyas*. The first is 'Aham Brahmasmi,'[134] which literally means, 'I am *Brahman*,' and can be translated as, 'I am God', or 'I am the truth', or 'I am the life', or 'I am the real.' The second great sentence is *'Tattvamasi'*.[135] Literally this means, 'That you are', which is to say, 'You are the truth', or 'You are the light', or 'You are the life', or 'You are the real.' The third great sentence is 'Ayatman Brahma',[136] which means, literally, 'Atman is Brahman', which can be understood as meaning, 'My real self is God', or 'I and God are one'. The fourth *mahavakhyas* is 'Sarvam etat Brahma',[137] which means, 'All this is *Brahman*', which is to say that although the whole created universe is limited by names and forms, it is essentially one with *Brahman*. Or one could say the whole universe is the manifestation of God. In this sense the whole universe, the whole of creation is also real, light, life and truth. There is also a *mahavakhya* that says, 'Prajnanam Brahman', that is, 'Brahman is consciousness.'[138] These *mahavakhyas* are mystical statements revealing eternal truth and should not be seen as intellectual propositions. They are liberating if understood properly but they either become a burden or we reject them if we misinterpret them.

The first of the *mahavakhyas*, 'Aham Brahmasmi', means, 'I am Brahman', or 'I am God'. If someone we knew came and said, 'I am God', it is likely that we would think that something was wrong with him or her. We have been taught that no human being can claim to be God and to say, 'I am God', is blasphemy. However, we have to ask which 'I' is making the statement. Is it the 'I' of the waking consciousness, the 'I' of the dreaming consciousness, the 'I' of the deep sleep consciousness, or the 'I' of *Thuriya*, the fourth state? The first three 'I' s are unreal, and only the fourth 'I' is real and only the fourth 'I' can make the statement. So this statement '*Aham Brahmasmi,*' is made only by the real 'I', which is God. So when a person says, 'I am God,' it actually means that he or she has realized that his or her real self is God, *Brahman*, light, life and so on. Instead of saying, 'I am God', it might be safer to say, 'My real I is *Brahman* or God'.

When a person discovers that his or her real 'I' is God, he or she discovers that the real 'you' of every human being is God, that the real self of every human being or creature is God, *Brahman*, truth, reality, light or life. Such a person then utters the second great statement, '*Tattvamasi,*' which means, 'You are that', or 'You are God.' Again we can ask which 'you' is being referred to? Just as there are four levels of 'I' there are four levels of 'you'. There is the 'you' of the waking consciousness, the 'you' of the dreaming consciousness, the 'you' of deep sleep consciousness and the 'you' of *Thuriya* which is God, truth and light. The first three levels of 'you' cannot be called God or real, only the fourth 'you' can be called God. So to say to someone, '*Tattvamasi*' – 'You are that' or 'You are God' – is to address the real 'you', who is God.

The liberating statement, '*Tattvamasi*', is complementary to, and a consequence of, the discovery of '*Aham Brahmasmi*'. A person who says, 'I have realized that I am *Brahman, Aham Brahmasmi,* but hereafter no other human being can have that experience, and everyone who is born in this world should prostrate themselves at my feet,' is an oppressor of humanity. But if a person says, 'I have discovered that my real "I" is God and I want everyone to discover this truth for themselves,' then such a person becomes a liberator or a redeemer.

The third *mahavakhyas* is '*Ayatman Brahma*', which means '*Atman* is *Brahman*', or 'I and God are one', or 'My real self is God'. The word *atman* refers to the foundation of individual consciousness and the word *Brahman* refers to the foundation of the universe, so the foundation of individual consciousness and the foundation of the universe are one and the same. Imagine a water tank fitted with many taps; each tap might individually say, 'My source is water', but it is really the same water. It is the same with reality. When reality is referred to as the foundation of an individual consciousness it is called '*atman*' and when it is referred to as the foundation of the universal consciousness it is called '*Brahman*'. The great sentence does not mean that the human soul is *Brahman* or that a human being is God, rather it means that the *atman* and *Brahman* are one and the same and to find the foundation of the universe, *Brahman*, we have to find the foundation of our inner being, *atman*.

The fourth *mahavakhya*, *sarvam etat Brahma* means that the whole creation is *Brahman* or God or truth. This statement can be thought to be pantheism but this would be incorrect. The Upanishads differentiate between the real and the unreal and acknowledge that God alone is real. There is only one God and one reality. Creation is not another reality apart from God, for this would mean there are two independent realities, each existing in their own right. This is not the understanding of the Upanishads. Creation is unreal but it is at the same time the unfolding of the divine, and as such it has a beginning and an end, it appears and disappears, but it is essentially one with the divine. When it appears and disappears it is called '*maya*' but in its real state it is one with the *Brahman* and is also eternal. Creation is the manifested or immanent aspect of reality. It is unreal or *maya* because it has a beginning and an end, a name and a form. *Maya* is that which can be measured, which has a beginning and an end. The Mandhukya Upanishad describes reality succinctly. *Om*. This eternal word is all – what was (the past), what is (the present) and what shall be (the future), and what is beyond in eternity (the transcendent). All is *om*; *om*, *Brahman* and *atman* are one and the same; creation is the man-ifested aspect of *om*, *Brahman* and *atman*.

One can think of God as the infinite ocean and of creation as a formation of ice upon the water. The water and the ice are not two independent realities, but one reality in two aspects, the formless and the form, the infinite and the finite. In the same way God and creation are two aspects of the one reality. When the ice knows that it is the manifestation of water, it is wisdom. But when the ice imagines that it is, as it were, a stone, it has fallen into the ignorance of wanting to become water though it is already water. In this way the ice creates the artifi-cial duality of water and the stone, and creates an artificial dis-tance between its reality as a stone and its ideal of being water. It invents, as it were, artificial means by which it might become the water, and creates the artificiality of religions and psycho-logical time.

How the eternal *Brahman* manifests this universe cannot be comprehended by the human mind and at this point the mind has to say, 'I do not know and I cannot know'. Semitic religions propose the theory of creation in which God created the world out of nothing, but this creation theory highlights the inade-quacy of the mind, which cannot explain the origin of creation. The limitation of the theory of creation is that it leaves no room for the experience of *advaita* or non-duality. When the relationship between God and creation is seen as *advaita* or 'non-duality', we can see that although creation appears to be finite, limited and transient, it is eternally one with *Brahman* and has eternal value.

The great sentences of the Upanishads reveal that there is only one reality, God or *Brahman* and that the foundation of human consciousness is identical with *Brahman*, does not *become Brahman* but is *already Brahman*. This is the Good News of the *mahavakhyas*. The four great statements are not four different experiences but only one experience communicated in four different statements. If we understand the insight of one of the great sentences we understand the insights of the others because each communicates the same experience or truth.

Chapter 19

Non-duality in the New Testament

The four stages in the development of humanity's relationship with God seen in the Vedic tradition are also found in the Biblical tradition. First there is the relationship with God through hymns, psalms, prayers and dance. Then there is the relationship with God through sacrifice of animals, birds, cereals and the like; there were innumerable varieties of sacrifice offered in the temple. In the third stage, the prophets, just like the sages of the Upanishad tradition, saw that God was not really interested in the sacrifice of bulls, goats and rams, and that all God wanted from humanity was a humble and contrite heart, an internal rather than an external sacrifice.

The prophets of the Old Testament saw that at some time in the future God would establish a new covenant, a new relationship with humanity in which he would take away our hearts of stone and give us hearts of flesh. Humanity would no longer have an external law but the law written in the heart. As we have seen, Jeremiah saw this clearly:

> This is the covenant which I will make with the house of Israel after these days,' says the Lord; 'I will put my law within them, and I will write it upon their hearts; and I will be their God, and they shall be my people.[139]

John the Baptist's move into the desert was the breakthrough of the Jewish consciousness in its relationship with God. He broke away from external religion leaving the well-established structure of the village and the town as he moved into the uninhabited desert, much as the sages of the Upanishads had gone into the forest centuries earlier. The desert is a place where there is no established path to follow, where there is no security, a place where one has to depend completely on the providence of God providing manna each day. John clearly saw that the old relationship with God was coming to an end and that the new relationship, the new covenant, was being inaugurated. In this sense John represents the *aranyaka* stage of the Vedic tradition, the stage in which there is a break with the past and in which there is no contact with eternal reality. John accepted that he was not the Messiah:

> I baptize you with water for repentance, but he who is coming after me is mightier than I, whose sandals I am not worthy to carry; he will baptize you with the Holy Spirit and with fire. His winnowing fork is in his hand, and he will clear his threshing floor and gather his wheat into the granary, but the chaff he will burn with unquenchable fire.[140]

The chaff can be seen as a symbol of the unreal, and the wheat as the symbol of the real, the eternal. So in burning the chaff Jesus purifies every relationship with God based on the impermanent, and establishes the relationship with the eternal. John the Baptist saw clearly that this new covenant was close at hand, here and now, in the person of Jesus. Jesus humbly invited John the Baptist to baptize him in the River Jordan whereupon Jesus experienced something which no other Jew had experienced before, which was beyond the expectation of any Jew and which did not exist in the Jewish memory. His experience of God went beyond even that of John; Jesus enters into

Thuriya, that fourth state of consciousness in which he discovered that he was 'the Son of God'.

> And when Jesus was baptized, he went up immediately from the water, and behold the heavens were opened and he saw the Spirit of God descending like a dove, and alighting on him; and Lo, a voice from heaven saying 'This is my beloved Son with whom I am well pleased.'[141]

As there was no precedent for this experience Jesus came into conflict with the religious tradition in which he had been brought up. In his direct experience of God, Jesus had to go beyond the relationship with God based on the old covenant and discover the new relationship based on the new covenant for so long promised by the prophets. He saw that his religious tradition was in need of repentance, that it needed to grow from a religion based on external law and the temple into a religion of the 'inner temple', the new covenant of the heart.

Jesus then communicated his experience of God through parables and through statements that came out of this experience. As with the *mahavakhyas* of the Upanishads these statements of Jesus point simply to his experience of himself as 'the Son of God'. These statements include 'I am the light of the world',[142] 'You are the light of the world',[143] 'I and the Father are one',[144] 'This is my body', 'This is my blood',[145] 'You are the salt of the earth',[146] 'I am the door',[147] 'I am',[148] 'I am the good shepherd',[149] and 'I am the way, the truth and the life'.[150] Understand one of these statements and you understand the others, and the whole of the gospel.

The statement, 'I am the light of the world', can be looked at in the light of the four levels of consciousness of the Upanishad tradition. We can ask which 'I' of Jesus can make this statement? There are four different 'I' s of Jesus; the first is the individual 'I' of Jesus as a human being, conditioned by his personal consciousness and his personal memory. The second 'I' is the dreaming consciousness of Jesus, conditioned by his Jewish identity, his Jewish memory and the spiritual tradition in which he had been raised. The third 'I' of Jesus is the 'I' of the deep sleep consciousness in which his personal memory and collective memory was open to the transcendent mystery of God, the experience of himself as the Son of the Father. In the silence of his Jewish consciousness Jesus discovered that he had God as the foundation of his consciousness; he discovered that he was the manifestation of the transcendent mystery. He used the words '*Abba*' or 'Father' and the word 'Son' to communicate the intimacy between the two 'I' s. However, these words and their meaning could not be understood within the Jewish tradition.

But Jesus had to go beyond even that level of consciousness in which he experienced himself and the Father as one. He realized that beyond his identity as the Son, beyond the 'I' of the Son, is the 'I' of the Father and that this 'I' of the Father is the light of the world. The 'I' of Jesus that said, 'I am the light of the world', is not any of the three unreal 'I' s, but the fourth, the *Thuriya*, in which the real 'I' is God, *Brahman*, truth, light, life, the God of the Upanishads. Jesus was saying that his real 'I' is the light of the world, that is to say, is God, and that he had no real existence outside God. Other statements such as, 'I am the truth', or 'I am the light', can be understood in the same way; it is God who made these statements for Jesus realized that his real self was God.

The realization of his own real self as God would have been incomplete had Jesus not also realized that the real self of every human being also is God, or the light of the world. So at the same time he was able to say, 'You are the light of the world,' realizing that this light, this awareness, is buried deep in the heart and humanity was not aware of it. So Jesus proclaimed, 'You are the light of the world but you have put that light under a bushel and are living in the darkness of ignorance.' He called upon his followers and the whole of humanity to 'realize that the light is buried with you. Put it on the stand and let it shine forth!' He told people that they were the 'salt of the earth' but that they had lost this consciousness with the consequence that the earth had lost its meaning and purpose.

Jesus did not say, 'You must become the light of the world,' or 'You must become the salt of the earth.' He was not telling people what they should *become* but what they *already were*; that they already were the salt of the earth and the light of the world, but that they did not realize it. If Jesus had told people that they had to *become* the salt of the earth or the light of the world he would have been placing an intolerable burden upon the shoulders of humanity and this would not have been good news, but bad news. The call of Jesus to every person is to real-ize who he or she already is in the depth of their heart, be aware of that which they have forgotten. This is the liberating mes-sage of Jesus.

When Jesus said, 'I and the Father are one', again it is not the limited or unreal 'I' of Jesus who is making the statement; it is his real 'I', the foundation of his human consciousness that in the Vedic tradition is called the *atman*. From his fourth level of consciousness Jesus was saying that his foundation was one with the Father, the source, the ground of the whole universe. This is just what the sages of the Upanishads had said centuries before when they realized that *atman*, the foundation of human consciousness, and *Brahman*, the foundation of the universe, are one and the same. Jesus' great statement, 'I and the Father are one', is almost identical with the statement of the Upanishads, '*Ayatman Brahman*' that is '*Atman is Brahman*'.

The eucharistic statement of Jesus, 'This is my body and this is my blood', also points to the reality that Jesus experienced at his baptism. When God said to Jesus at his baptism, 'You are my beloved son', he was proclaiming the eucharistic words that Jesus was indeed the body and blood of God. The Jesus to whom God was referring was not the individual Jesus, the Jew, but the Jesus who is the whole humanity and the whole creation. God was speaking to the whole of creation and was saying that the whole creation is the son or the daughter of God, the whole of creation is the body and blood of God, the whole creation is nothing but the manifestation of God.

By entering into the divine consciousness Jesus had seen the real nature of creation, and had realized that just as he was the body and blood of God, the whole of creation was the body and blood of God. He was able to see the image of God or the 'kingdom of God' in every particle of the manifested world. He saw little children being suckled and said that the kingdom of God is like that, he saw a woman putting yeast in flour and said that the kingdom of God is like that. Whatever he saw, he saw one reality – which he called the kingdom of God.

Scientists have discovered that matter and energy are two aspects of the same reality, that energy is the one reality and matter is the 'solidification' of this energy. In the same way Jesus discovered spiritually that God is the only reality and that creation is the manifestation, or solidification, of this reality in space and time. The same understanding is found in the Upanishads that say, '*Sarvametat Brahma*', or, 'All this is a manifestation of God'. When Jesus said, 'This is my body and this is my blood,' he was saying, 'Just as I and the Father are one, so also I and the whole of creation are one. Though this bread and wine appear to be different and separate from me, we are one. Just as I am in the Father and the Father is in me, so also you are in me and I am in you, I am in creation and creation is in me. Ultimately God and I are one, you and I are one, creation and I are one.' The eucharistic words are a statement of Christian non-duality; to eat his body and drink his blood is to become one with him, to become one with the creation and to become one with God.

Jesus shared the realization of his unity with God and with creation when he told his disciples he was sharing his body and blood with them. He told them to do the same in memory of him, inviting them to experience this truth themselves, not just as an external repetition but as an internal realization, and in so doing help others towards the same realization. In saying, 'This is my body and this is my blood', Jesus was revealing eternal truth just as God the Father revealed his eternal truth to him with the words, 'This is my beloved son'.

Whilst Jesus was clear about his *identity* with the Father as the ground of his consciousness he also made it clear that there is *relationship* between the Father and the Son. The Father is seen as greater than the Son. The Son is the one in whom the Father does his work.

> Do you not believe that I am in the Father and the Father is in me? The words that I say to you I do not speak on my own authority; but the Father who dwells in me does his works. Believe me that I am in the Father and the Father in me, or else believe me for the sake of the works themselves.[151]

Jesus said that he will 'go to the Father',[152] that he will 'pray to the Father',[153] that the 'Father is greater than he',[154] and that he does 'what the Father commands' him to do and that he 'loves the Father.'[155] 'Abba, Father, all things are possible to thee; remove this cup from me, yet not what I will but what thou wilt.'[156] 'My God, my God, why hast thou forsaken me?'[157] All these statements imply a certain duality, a certain separation and a certain gradation.

The experience of identity and the experience of relationship do not contradict each other. The experience of non-duality at the fourth level of consciousness, the *Thuriya* of the Upanishads, is the point of arrival in the ascending order of the human consciousness, but one then has to come down again to the ordinary human experience and relate to the external world and to people in the world of duality. The third level of deep-sleep consciousness is the state of 'ego-lessness' in which the movement of the past, the movement of both personal and collective memory, has stopped. This level of consciousness receives its inspiration from the ultimate reality, and at the same time uses memory to communicate through external relationships as well as with God. It is this center that calls God 'Father' and says, 'I am in the Father and the Father is in me. The words that I speak are not my own but the Father who dwells in me does his works.' These words of Jesus imply ontological unity and communion with the Father whilst implying a functional duality at the same time. The experience of Jesus as being one with the Father, whilst at the same time being separate, enables the human consciousness to experience itself as a created being while at the same time seeing itself as God. To be identical with God at the ontological level and to act dualistically in the world of creation is the miracle of life.

Jesus' words, 'I am the Way, the Truth and the Life', are another expression of the relationship of non-duality.

Traditionally, this statement has been interpreted to mean that Jesus is the only way to God. He is the truth and the life and there is no other way to salvation. Jesus Christ is the only saviour, and outside Christ there is no salvation and Christianity is the only way to salvation. The words 'way', 'truth' and 'life' all refer to the one reality, that is, God who is truth and life. When Jesus said, 'I am the truth' and 'I am the life' we should not identify the 'I' of Jesus with his limited and unreal 'I'. The 'I' of Jesus making this statement is his real 'I' who, as we have seen, is God. Jesus was saying, 'My real "I" who is God is the way, the truth and the life.' The real 'I' of Jesus, as the universal consciousness in which all of humanity is present, is the way the truth and the life. The word 'way' implies a road or a path, conditioned by time and space, which has a beginning and which moves towards a particular point in the future. However, as we have seen, the radical message of Jesus is about the *end of all ways*, that *there is no way to God*.

The great sentences, the *mahavakhyas*, of Jesus all reflect the experience Jesus had of his unity with God and with creation at the deepest level of his being. If we understand just one of these great sentences we understand the others and the whole of his teaching.

Chapter 20

The Lord's Prayer

'As long as you are aware that you are praying, you are not praying,' goes a saying of the desert fathers. Awareness of praying
creates duality between God and ourselves and in the ultimate
state of prayer there is no duality, no dualistic awareness for, as
we have seen, the divine-human relationship is non-dualistic,
the human self is self-less self. Grace is union with God; it is the
realization that God is the only absolute reality and that we
have no reality apart from God. A Sufi mystic, referring to the
experience of the separated self, said, 'My greatest sin is my own
existence.' Sin is a falling away of our awareness from the real
to the unreal, from light to darkness and from immortality to
death, that is to say, from eternity into time. Our experience
that we are separate from God is not real but is unreal, is not
absolute but relative. Thus the deepest longing of the human
heart has been described in the Vedic prayer:

> Lead me from the Unreal to the Real
> From Darkness to Light
> From Death to Immortality.

Jesus taught the disciples to pray the *Our Father*. The richness
and the mystery of this prayer can never be exhausted. Millions
of people have prayed it, experienced it, interpreted it and mil-

lions will do so in the future. In the light of Jesus' experience of God as his real self we can say that in praying the *Our Father* we are asking God to purify our ego, to make our ego a self-less ego so that it becomes a transparent instrument of divine grace and love.

Our Father in Heaven: The word 'Father' conveys the intimate relationship Jesus had with God whom he could boldly call, '*Abba*, Father'. The word has its limitations as it excludes the feminine or motherhood aspect of God, but in experiencing God as Father, Jesus experienced God as the only reality, the source, and he realized that God is more intimate to us than we are to ourselves. Jesus realized that in his manifested self he was not real as the Father is real, but at the same time he was aware that he was one with, or equal with, the Father in the source just as the sun's rays are not equal to the sun in their manifested state, yet they are one with the sun in the source.

To call God 'Father' is to be aware of our relative reality and see that God is the only absolute reality. It is a state of enlightenment. Although there appears to be many sons and daughters of God in the world, when a person comes closer to God, he or she realizes that there is only one Son or one Daughter, and that the one Son or Daughter is not 'I' but 'we'. So he or she cannot call God 'his father' or 'her father' but only 'our Father'. The word 'heaven' refers to our one source who is God and should not be understood as a place somewhere in the sky.

Holy is your name: This means, 'Let your name be sanctified', or 'Let your name be glorified'. God is holy, holiness personified and is whole or wholeness. Nothing can be added to God and nothing can be taken from God. By creating the world, God does not get anything more, and by not creating he does not lose anything. Only God's own actions are holy and whole whereas human actions are unholy and un-whole, arising from motivation, a sense of insufficiency and out of desire. Human actions are fragmentary, in that sin is fragmentation and a fragmented action yields fragmented results, a sinful action produces sin. The action of God liberates us from our fragmentation.

Jesus was aware of the nature of human action and was aware that however great it may be, an action has no eternal value if it does not come from God. It will be lost in the process of time. Many great movements have come into this world and they have all disappeared in time. There have been great reformations, and they have all disappeared. Jesus was always careful not to fall from eternal action so he taught his disciples to be on guard and asked them to pray for liberation from the fragmentary action of the fallen self. People will see only the action of God in a person who is free from fragmentation and they will praise the name of God.

God has no name or form, for these limit the nature of God. The name of God is one with the being of God, which is 'holy' and 'whole'. The fragmentary self cannot even utter the name of God, so Jesus asked his disciples to pray to be free from the state of fragmentation, from un-holiness and from un-wholeness and to be in contact with wholeness and holiness, so that God's name might be glorified.

Your Kingdom come: The kingdom of God is not a place in time and space; it is the 'being' of God, the relational aspect in which God's power is experienced. The rule of God is the rule of wholeness and the rule of holiness unifying humanity and creation. The rule of the ego is the rule of sin, fragmentation and un-holiness; it is a rule that divides and creates conflict. The 'unity' that we experience through the ego is artificial, based on beliefs, ideas, convictions and experiences that can be changed at any time, whereas the unity of the kingdom of God is not artificial; it is an essential unity. The nature of the ego is that it always has an enemy to fight. The rule of God has no enemy for there is no reality apart from God. It does not fight just as the light does not fight with the darkness. When light dawns, darkness disappears. The coming of the kingdom of God means the end of the rule of the ego, the rule of fragmentation, the rule of sin. The rule of God is absolute and eternal whereas the rule of the ego is relative and temporal. Only when the ego realizes that all efforts to perpetuate itself are futile does it surrender itself to the kingdom of God. Then the kingdom of God is manifested in and through the ego, which then becomes an instrument of God's kingdom.

Thy will be done on Earth as in Heaven: Will is the source of guidance, the source of commitment and the source of power. But it is also the source of conflict, and the source of division. Will divides to form 'my will' and 'God's will'. God's being and God's will are one and the same. We cannot say that God has a will as an adjunct to 'my will'. The will of God does not project God into the essential future, it does not create psychological time, for in God there is no psychological past nor future, God is always present in the here and the now. Since God's 'being' and his will are one and the same, the will of God is always 'done' in heaven, where there is no time gap between God's will and its fulfillment. God wills a thing and it happens. God's will is its own simultaneous fulfillment.

Jesus asked the disciples to pray that God's will be done on *Earth*. Earth can be taken to be a symbol of the ego, the world of space and time where there is a gap between willing and fulfilling, the world of time where there is past, present and future. Where there is time there is conflict – my will and God's will. Jesus asked his disciples to pray that the will of God is done on earth, that the will of the earth, the ego, should come to an end. We can see millions of wills and millions of egos in the world, but these egos are manifestations of that universal ego that is the fallen self, the fallen Adam, fallen humankind that thinks it is a reality independent of God.

According to the Indian sages, the greatest human being is not the one who has done wonderful things in the world, but the one who has conquered, or rather silenced, his or her ego, and who has surrendered his or her human will to God. Jesus said, 'I have not come to do my own will but the will of God who sent me.' Just as the rule of God is the rule of wholeness and holiness, so also the will of God is the will of wholeness and holiness. This will of God is our sanctification, it makes us holy and whole and redeems us from sin and fragmentation. This is only possible when the human will realizes that it is only relative and surrenders itself to God, the absolute.

Give us this day our daily bread: This can be understood as material food necessary for our physical nourishment or as spiritual food necessary for our spiritual nourishment. We can accumulate enough material food for many days ahead and then stay at home and eat. We don't need to work every day. But in the spiritual plane God is beyond time and lives in the eternal present. God only gives for now, today, for tomorrow does not exist for

God. When God was leading the Israelites out of Egypt he fed the people with manna, and they were told to collect sufficient for each day. Similarly, in our relationship with God, we receive sufficient spiritual food for our present need, and it is not to be accumulated for the future.

Accumulation distorts both the future and the present. To see the present as it really is we have to be 'empty' or poor in spirit. When we are 'empty' we are obedient, that is, we see the truth as it is today and not as it is conditioned by the past or the future. When we see the truth as it is today we are able to make a chaste relationship with God, with the truth. Our life is the life of the ego, the life of time, the life of the past entering into and contaminating the present, and the present moving into and contaminating the future. True obedience is to see what God is today and not what God was or will be. If we continue to hold onto something of what we receive today, we see God tomorrow with the eyes of today. In the same way revelations are not to be accumulated but experienced and consumed today so that we are 'empty' and ready for tomorrow's new revelations.

A wandering *sannyasi* begins each day with an empty bowl and collects food only for that day. In the spiritual plane the *sannyasi* is supposed to be like an empty bowl. The difficulty is that we tend to collect more than is necessary, so that we are living in the past rather than in the present. It is only when we live in the present that we live in the kingdom of God. We have to ask God each moment of our life to give us our daily bread, and only our daily bread. We have to ask God to help us not to accumulate and to help us not to create ego, the source of sin. When we are empty we live in the present moment, in the now.

Forgive us our sins: Sins are the manifestation of *sin*, which is nothing other than our separation from God. Our greatest sin is to think that we are independent of God, for our separated self or fallen self is the source of sin. Because humanity is one and we all participate in that humanity, Jesus asked the disciples to pray to God for forgiveness from *sin*, the source of all sins. When God forgives *sin* all sins are forgiven.

So that we forgive those who sin against us: When we experience universal *sin*, that source of all sins, within ourselves, and when we receive forgiveness from that *sin*, we not only experience God's forgiveness for ourselves but also for the whole of humanity. This is because our deepest self is not the individual 'I' but the universal 'we'. When we forgive others we are forgiving ourselves, rather we are announcing the forgiveness of God in and through us. We have experienced God's forgiveness for them in us. So when we forgive our neighbors it is not really we who are forgiving, but God himself.

Do not bring us to the test: The experience of test or temptation belongs to the world of duality. As God is the only absolute reality and there is no other reality apart from God, the created world has only relative reality in which there is duality and temptation, the world of time and space, the world of the ego and conflict. It is only by taking us above the level of duality that God can save us from this situation. It is only by transcending our human will, our ego and the world of duality that we can escape from this situation. It is only by this spiritual process that we can enter the kingdom of God.

Our greatest difficulty is that we are always prone to create a separated self, materially, psychologically and spiritually.

There is a positive aspect to temptations or tests in that they reveal to us our separation. We can look upon them as guardian angels, who protect us from falling, from creating a separated self. Where there is separation there is temptation; where there is no separation there is no temptation. When we ask God not to bring us to the test we are asking God to free us from our fallen state, the state of separation, and to bring us to unity or oneness or union with him.

Deliver us from evil: Evil is not an absolute reality for God is the only absolute reality. Evil belongs to the world of duality and relative reality. The source of evil is our fallen self, our desire to become like God. We can say that evil comes into being when relative reality assumes that it is absolute reality. In the language of the Indian sages, it is the unreal thinking that is the real, ignorance thinking that it is light, and death thinking that it is life. But the unreal cannot become real, darkness cannot become light and death cannot become life. As long as we are cut off from the source of all things, we are in the world of good and evil, the world of duality. Once we realize this fact and surrender our ego to God, our actions are no longer of the ego but of the real, the truth and the life, which is the kingdom of God. So when we ask God to deliver us from evil we are asking God to deliver us from being centered on our ego, our false self.

The essence of the Lord's Prayer is asking God to liberate us from our fallen state of being in the ego and separate from God. Each request made in the Lord's Prayer is full in itself and refers to the same need to be free from our separateness. This is the prayer that we have to make each moment of our life. Jesus said, 'Watch and pray that you may not enter into temptation,' so we have to be watchful and prayerful, for if we don't we fall into a state of separation.

Prayer is the movement of the life of the ego into the life of God and with this in mind we can say the Our Father in the language of the Indian sages:

Our Father in Heaven	The Source of our Being
Holy be your name	Lead us from un-holiness to holiness
Your kingdom come	From fragmentation to wholeness
Your will be done on earth as in heaven	From conflict to harmony
Give us today our daily bread	From time to eternity
Forgive us our sins as we forgive those who sin against us	From sin to grace
Do not bring us to the test	From duality to unity
But deliver us from evil	From darkness to light

Notes

Chapter 1
The Good News
[1] Mark 1:15
[2] Matthew 4:17
[3] Matthew 4:9
[4] John 6:14-15
[5] Matthew 20:20-23
[6] Matthew 16:21-23
[7] Luke 24:21
[8] Acts 1:6-7
[9] 1 Thessalonians 4:14,16
[10] 2 Peter 3:4
[11] 2 Peter 3:8
[12] Revelation 20:1-6
[13] Luke 17:20-21

Chapter 2
The experience of the kingdom of God
[14] Matthew 12:24-28
[15] John 14:8-11
[16] Matthew 13:44
[17] Matthew 13:45-46
[18] Matthew 13:47-50
[19] Mark 4:31-32
[20] Mark 4:26-29
[21] Matthew 13:33
[22] Matthew 20:1-16
[23] Luke 16:1-8

Chapter 3
Humanity searches for God and God searches for humanity
[24] Luke 15:4-7
[25] Luke 15:8-10
[26] Luke 15:17-20
[27] Luke 19:7
[28] Luke 19:9-10
[29] Luke 7:31-35
[30] Luke 9:58

Chapter 4
Blessed are the poor
[31] John 3:3
[32] Luke 12:13-21
[33] Luke 12:33
[34] Luke 18:22
[35] Mark 1:16-20
[36] Luke 9:23-25
[37] Luke 9:58
[38] Luke 9:59
[39] Luke 9:60
[40] Luke 9:61-62
[41] Mark 2:18-19
[42] Mark 2:20
[43] Mark 2:21-22
[44] Mark 2:14
[45] Mark 2:16-17
[46] Luke 7:39

Chapter 5
Spiritual and intellectual poverty
[47] Luke 9:58
[48] Luke 18:9-14
[49] Luke 6:24
[50] Luke 14:15-24
[51] Matthew 21:28-32
[52] Matthew 19:24
[53] Matthew 10:34-39
[54] Matthew 18:1-4
[55] Matthew 11:25-26
[56] Matthew 11:28-30

Chapter 6
For they will be comforted; they will inherit the earth
[57] John 5:26
[58] John 10:10

59 Luke 9:54-56
60 Luke 20:10-16

Chapter 7
Blessed are those who hunger
61 John 3:1-8
62 John 4:1-26
63 Mark 8:11-12
64 Mark 12:14-17
65 Luke 20:28-33
66 Luke 20:34-40
67 Luke 10:25-37
68 Matthew 12:1-2
69 Matthew 12:9-10
70 Matthew 12:38-39

Chapter 8
Blessed are the merciful
71 Luke 6:37-38
72 Mark 4:24
73 Matthew 7:3-5
74 Luke 15:11-24
75 John 8:6-11

Chapter 9
Blessed are the pure in heart,
the peacemakers and the persecuted
76 Luke 11:34-36
77 Exodus 3:13-15
78 Matthew 5:9
79 John 14:27
80 John 16:33
81 Matthew 5:10

Chapter 10
The cage becomes a nest
82 Jeremiah 31:32-33
83 John 1:17
84 Mark 2:21-22

85 John 4:23-24
86 Matthew 5:20
87 Matthew 11:28-30
88 Luke 11:46
89 Luke 11:52
90 Luke 4:18-19

Chapter 11
Jesus walks on the water
91 Matthew 14:24-25
92 John 15:15
93 Matthew 23:8-12
94 John 5:26
95 John 10:10
96 Matthew 26:33
97 Matthew 16:17-19
98 Matthew 7:13-14
99 John 1:36

Chapter 12
Who do you say that I am?
100 Luke 9:18-20
101 Luke 9:20; Mark 8:29
102 Matthew 16:16
103 Matthew 16:17
104 Luke 9:22
105 Matthew 16:23
106 John 10:30
107 John 8:58
108 Matthew 11:25-26

Chapter 13
The Virgin, the child and the
wise men
109 Matthew 1:23; Isaiah 7:14
110 Matthew 2:10-11
111 Matthew 2:1-2
112 Matthew 2:9-10
113 Matthew 2:1-3
114 Matthew 2:12
115 Matthew 2:13

Chapter 14
Preach the gospel to all creation
[116] John 8:12
[117] Matthew 5:14
[118] Matthew 5:13
[119] Matthew 11:28-30
[120] John 12:24
[121] Mark 16:16
[122] Matthew 6:33

Chapter 15
Creative life and prayer
[123] Matthew 22:17
[124] John 8:4-5
[125] Luke 18:18-20
[126] John 3:3-6
[127] John 1:17
[128] John 1:12-13
[129] John 3:6-8
[130] Matthew 26:39

Chapter 17
A new vision of Christianity
[131] Pantheism means that everything *is* God; Panentheism means that God *is in* everything
[132] Jeremiah 31:33-34
[133] Luke 4:18-19

Chapter 18
Non-duality in the Upanishads
[134] Brhadaranyaka Upanishad 1, 4, 10
[135] Chandogya Upanishad 6, 8, 7
[136] Mandukhya Upanishad 2
[137] Mandukhya Upanishad 2
[138] Aitareya Upanishad 5, 3

Chapter 19
Non-duality in the New Testament
[139] Jeremiah 31:33-34
[140] Matthew 3:11-12
[141] Matthew 3:16-17
[142] John 8:12
[143] Matthew 5:14
[144] John 10:30
[145] Matthew 26:26,28
[146] Matthew 5:13
[147] John 10:9
[148] John 8:24, 28, 58; John 13:19
[149] John 10:14
[150] John 14:6
[151] John 14:10-11; John 10:38
[152] John 14:12
[153] John 14:16
[154] John 14:28
[155] John 14:31
[156] Mark 14:36
[157] Mark 15:34